JN409129

한영희 시집
The Collection of Young Hee Han's Poems
한영대역판
Korean-English Edition

무도회의 풍경
Scene of Ball

예라蘂羅 한 영 희
Young Hee Han
(Nom de plume: Yera)

다솜출판사

Poet's Words

I have liked writing since my childhood.
It was because I could live in innocence and run to the distant future.

Although I liked writing, to this day I believe writing is the most difficult of undertakings. This thought should be an awareness that everyone possesses.

However, despite all of its challenges, I am most happy when I am writing. Thus, I cannot ever give it up.

I am ashamed that I have come to publish my first collection of poems only now, in the later years of my life, after the passage of many years since I became a poet. However, although I am clumsy and weak now, I will strive hereafter to become a poet who can create extraordinary impressions through my efforts. I would like to be remembered by many people; it is my aim to be remembered for a long time through my words, and the love and passion that I weave through them.

시인의 말

나는 어린 시절부터 글쓰기를 좋아했습니다
동심에서 살기도 하고 먼 미래로 달려갈 수 있기 때문이었습니다.

내가 글쓰기를 좋아했지만, 가장 어려운 것도 글쓰기임을 오늘날까지 느끼며 살아왔습니다. 이러한 생각은 누구나 다 갖는 의식일 것입니다.

내가 포기 할 수 없는 것이 글이기에 글을 쓸 때가 가장 행복한 시간이 되었습니다.

시인이 된 지 수년이 지나 이제야 겨우 첫 시집을 내게 되어 부끄럽기 까지 합니다. 그러나 지금은 서툴고 미약하나 앞으로 많은 노력으로 남다른 감동을 만들어 낼 수 있는 시인이 되고자 노력할 것입니다. 많은 분들께 오랫동안 기억되도록 하고 싶습니다. 그래서 뒷모습이 아름다운 작가가 되고 싶은 욕심도 있습니다.

My first published collection of poems is called, “Scene of Ball.” I earnestly thank Professor Emeritus Dr. Won Chul Choi of Pusan National University for his help. When he gave a lecture on poetry, the story of, “The World I Cannot Know”, was like a waltz with intelligence capable of inspiring greatness. I would also like to express my thanks to my colleagues who studied with me and supported me.

In particular, I am truly grateful to my husband, who has always considered me generously with his love or financially. And I would like to express my gratitude to my daughter and son, who grew up well, met each other's spouses, and started new families.

March, 2024

Young Hee Han

"무도회의 풍경"이라고 첫 시집을 상재하고자 합니다. 여기에 도움을 주신 부산대학교 최원철 명예 교수님께 진심으로 감사드립니다. 시에 대한 강의를 해주실 때 "내가 알 수 없는 세계"의 이야기는 위대한 작품을 만들어낼 수 있는 지성의 왈츠와 같았습니다.
또한 함께 공부하며 응원해 주신 여러 동료 선생님들께도 감사드리고 싶습니다.

특히, 한결같이 사랑으로, 혹은 경제적으로, 아낌없이 배려해 준 남편께 진심으로 감사한 마음을 가지고 있습니다. 그리고, 반듯하게 잘 자라 서로의 배우자 만나 새 가정을 꾸민 딸, 아들에게 고마움을 전하고자 합니다.

2024년 3월

한 영 희

Profile

Young Hee Han

(Nom de plume: Yera)

- Graduated Kyungsung University
- Completed the CEO course at Kyungsung University
- Completed the Advanced Management Program of Graduate School of Business, Pusan National University
- Reporter, UBC Welfare TV, Buulgyeong Broadcasting Co., Ltd. Division of News & Sports
- Debut as a poet of City of Literature (Busan Writers Association)
- Member of City of Literature (Busan Writers Association)
- Member of New Busan Poets Association
- Secretary of Poetry and Literature, Yangsan City Cultural Center,
- Gyeongsangnam-do
- Current Managing Director of Samyoung Co., Ltd.

예라(蘂羅) **한영희**

- 경성대학교 졸업
- 경성대학교 CEO과정 수료
- 부산대학교 경영대학원 최고경영자과정 수료
- UBC 복지 TV 부울경 방송(주) 보도본부 기자
- 부산광역시 문인협회 (사)부산문인협회 월간<문학도시> 시분야 등단
- 부산광역시 문인협회 (사)부산문인협회 회원
- 새부산 시인협회 회원
- 경남 양산시 문화원 시문학반 사무국장
- 現 ㈜삼영 관리이사

Contents ••• 목차

Comma of Summer II 여름의 쉼표

When Hungry for Life III 삶에 허기질 때

Four-o'clock, My Elder Sister  분꽃 언니

Scene of a Ball
V
무도회의 풍경

Chapter 1
Countryside at the Break of Dawn

제1장
새벽을 여는 시골

Countryside at the Break of Dawn

When the darkness clears up,
A sound that tells dawn from a distance
The grass eliminator is rotating.
When the sound of the bull's bell is heard,
I open my eyes at the sound of roosters crowing at dawn.

In a dawning morning carrying freshness,
After putting aside shallow ideas in front of nature.
I listen to the language of the universe in silence.

When the morning outing begins,
Ggamsuni in the house next door talks with her tail.
The dawn in the countryside is just affectionate.

When dawn comes in the countryside, even poetry begins
to wake up from sleep.

새벽을 여는 시골

어둠이 걷히면
멀리에서 새벽을 알리는 소리
예초기가 돌아가고
황소의 방울 소리가 들리면
새벽닭 우는 소리에 눈을 뜬다.

상쾌함을 나르는 동트는 아침
자연 앞에서 얕은 생각일랑 접고
침묵 속에서 우주의 언어를 듣는다

아침 나들이가 시작되면
꼬리로 말하는 윗집 깜 순이
시골의 새벽이 정겹기만 하다

시골의 새벽이 되면 시詩도 잠에서 깨어나기 시작한다

A Day of Farmers

In summer when
Rain clouds roll
To pour a shower of rain

The rain falling on the vegetable garden
Quickens the farmers' hand movements that have been slow and slight
To make the working hands busy

Sometimes, to avoid the rain
When I hide at the edge of eaves
A leisurely rural scene comes to mind.

In hot weather
While drinking a cup of tea under the shade
When a cloud has passed by
A farmer's leisurely life begins the day

농사꾼의 하루

비구름 몰려와 한줄기
쏟아 붓는
여름

텃밭에 내리는 비는
꼼지락거리던 손놀림을 빠르게 움직이게 하여
일손을 바쁘게 한다

가끔, 비를 피해
처마 끝에 숨어들면
여유로운 시골의 풍경이 그려진다

뜨거운 날씨에는
그늘 밑에서 차 한 잔 마시며
구름 한 점 지나가면
농사꾼의 여유로운 하루의 삶이 시작된다

Banquet Noodles at a Rural Market

Having fresh greens
In the countryside fifth-day market
Sellers are generous

The smell of a country market that has been familiar since ancient times
Of the savory anchovy stock
Crisscrosses the alleys of the fifth-day market

Placed on fine noodles
Stir-fried in sesame oil
Pumpkin garnish
Slurp, the noodles are eaten like a storm in an instant.

When I emptied a bowl of noodles
The ample satiety for 5,000 won
Makes me happy

Before I know

시골장의 잔치국수

싱싱한 푸성귀가 있는
시골 오일장
인심이 두둑하다

예부터 익숙한 시골 장터 냄새는
구수한 멸칫국물로
오일장의 골목 안을 누빈다

고운 면발에 얹어 놓은
참기름에 볶아 낸
낭개의 고명
후루룩 삽시간에 폭풍 흡입이 일어난다

국수 한 그릇 비우면
오천 원에 두둑한 포만감은
나를 기쁘게 한다

There is a long line of people in front of the tasty restaurant.

When I was late only 5 minutes, I would miss the happy taste
Sometimes I was startled.

Exchanged at the countryside market
The warm heart
Makes even the cold weather warm

어느덧
맛집 앞에는 사람들의 줄이 길다

5분만 늦었으면 행복한 맛을
놓칠까 아찔할 때도 있었다

시골 장에서 주고받는
따뜻한 마음은
차가운 날씨조차 훈훈하게 한다

Rainy Morning

One longing hung
On the sky with dark, black clouds
Becomes monsoon rain to fall

Unforgettable rain
Burrows deep into my heart
To shake my longing

Even when the morning has come
My body is soaked with longing in my dreams
I can't shake off the longing all over my body.

In my moist eyes
Completely transformative welcome rain
Falls
Balmily on a summer morning

비 내리는 아침

시커먼 먹구름 하늘에
걸어 둔 그리움 하나
장맛비 되어 내린다

잊을 수 없는 비
마음속까지 파고들어
보고픔을 흔든다

아침이 되어도
꿈속에서 그리움에 적셔진 나의 몸
온 몸에 보고픔은 떨칠 수 없다

촉촉이 젖은 눈망울에
감쪽같이 변신한 단비가
여름 아침에 상쾌하게
내리고 있다

Spring That Comes Slowly

Petals tensed up due to the cold
Like the faces of pretty maidens
Sulkily stick their heads out

Flowers of different colors on the same branch
To bloom or not to bloom?
The flower tree falls into agony

At the moment when the flower tree is about to draw a beautiful season
One raindrop
Comes down
On the branch of the flower tree where spring comes

Before the season that is stretching
What should I do!
Borderless COVID-19
Looks at the flowers exposed to the spring rain

더디게 오는 봄

추위로 긴장한 꽃잎은
예쁜 처녀의 얼굴처럼
뽀로통하게 고개를 내민다

같은 가지에서 다른 색깔의 꽃들이
필 것인가, 말 것인가?
꽃나무는 고뇌에 빠진다

아름다운 계절을 그리려는 순간
빗방울 하나가
봄이 오는 꽃나무 가지에
내려앉는다

기지개를 켜는 계절 앞에
어찌할까!
국경 없는 코로나19가
봄비 맞는 꽃들을 쳐다본다

The Day of the First Full Moon of the Lunar Year

Under the moonlight startled by the sound of biting on a nut to ward off boils
A glass of ear-quickening wine to give away the heat
The memories of drinking it happily are fresh.

Five-grain rice with seasoned wild vegetables
Stew with frozen pollack and tofu
Sunshine and wind falling on the top of the mountain
Children running around dropping leaves
The day of the first full moon of the lunar year is gradually getting busier.

When the season that brought the warm breeze
Hung spring on a tree
A warm affection seeps into my heart.

Built a bonfire
Performed a ritual to Earth God viewing the moon
Beating a gong

Signaled the day of the first full moon of the lunar year
The old days are missed today

정월대보름

부름 깨무는 소리에 놀란 달빛 아래
더위를 팔던 귀밝이술 한잔
기쁘게 마시던 추억이 새롭다

오곡밥에 산채나물
동태에 두부 넣은 찌게
산꼭대기에 내리는 햇살과 바람
잎새를 떨구며 나대던 아이들
대보름은 점점 바빠진다

훈풍을 몰고 온 계절이
나무에 봄을 매달면
내 마음에는 따스한 정이 스민다

모닥불 피워놓고
달맞이에 지신 밟고
꽹과리 두드리며
정월대보름을 알리던

옛날이 그리운 오늘이다

Boiled Egg

Holding a round basket
They shout all day long
Is that a shout for survival?
Or a shout to eat?

There are cider, tangerines, and boiled eggs.
In the night train, the voices of merchants
Spread throughout the room

The sounds of shouting and touting
I want to hear more
But as time passed
They are not seen at all these days

In boiled eggs
Even if the yolk and white are clearly distinguished,
There are no peeping sounds of chicks
That will come out into the wide world

The dynamic sound of life roiling
I hope the foundations of life are full of it

삶은 계란

둥근 바구니 하나
종일 들고 외친다
살기 위한 외침일까?
먹기 위한 외침일까?

사이다, 밀감, 삶은 계란이 있어요
밤 기차에 상인들의 목소리가
객실에 퍼져나간다

외치는 호객행위 소리를
더 듣고 싶지만
시간이 흘러
요즘 아예 볼 수 없다

삶은 계란에는
노른자와 흰자가 뚜렷하게 구별되어도
그 속에는 넓은 세상에 나올
삐약대는 병아리 소리가 없다

생명이 요동치는 역동적인 소리
삶의 터전에 가득했으면 좋겠다

Walk Following the Starlight

To the house of happiness seen far away
Amicably with each other, my heart and legs
Are walking

Until the end of life
When a dark night will come
So that neither moonlight
Nor starlight will be visible
I will walk even a dark road

Following the fragrance of flowers in full bloom
Although a long but short journey
In loneliness and joy
Following the starlight twinkling in the dark sky
I am still walking beautifully along the road

별빛 따라 걷는다

저 멀리 보이는 행복의 집으로
마음과 다리는 서로 의좋게
걷고 있다

달빛도
별빛도 보이지 않는
어두운 밤이 찾아오는
생의 마지막까지
캄캄한 길이라도 걸어야겠다

활짝 핀 꽃의 향내를 따라
길고도 짧은 여행이지만
외로움과 환희 속에서
어두운 하늘에 반짝이는 별빛 따라
지금도 아름답게 길을 걷고 있다

Kimchi Stew

In the pot
Embracing each other, temperature and seasonings
A whispering sound is heard

Being cooked well
Means
That the body and mind are mixed well

As time goes by
As the sound of spoons hitting each other
Is heard from inside the pot
Into our hearts
Seeps warm love

김치 찌게

냄비 안에서
온도와 양념이 서로 껴안고
속삭이는 소리가 들린다

잘 익어간다는 것은
몸과 마음이 잘 버무려진다는
의미이다

시간이 흐를수록
숟가락이 서로 부딪히는 소리가
냄비 속에서 들리면
우리네 마음에
따뜻한 사랑이 스미게 된다

Winter Solstice

Without a break nights and days
Run stealthily

When the twelfth month of the lunar year
Is rooted in winter like a stalactite,
Red bean porridge is boiling in the kitchen.

When smoke left a few soot marks
On the cast iron cauldron
The heat hides its tail

When the moon hides
With its back to the sun far away
Today comes running like a shot arrow

When the sun shines
The shy daytime moon that appears like a shadow
Walks carefully
Alone...lonelily

동짓날

밤과 낮이 쉼 없이
슬금슬금 달려간다

동지선달이
종유석처럼 겨울에 뿌리박고 있을 때
팥죽은 부엌에서 끓고 있다

무쇠솥에 연기가
그을음을 몇 점 남긴 채
꼬리를 감추는 열기

저 멀리 태양을 등지고
달이 숨을 때
쏜살같이 달려오는 오늘

태양이 빛날 때
그림자처럼 나타나는 수줍은 낮달
혼자서 외로이
조심스레 걸어간다

Tomorrow when a new sun
Stands up with a powerful resurrection
A new year begins again

내일은 새로운 태양이
힘찬 부활로 일어서면
다시 새해가 시작된다

Happy Meal

When the curtain is drawn aside
Savory steamed multigrain rice wrapped
In pumpkin leaves and topped with soybean paste
Welcomes me

Ripening in *ssams*
Refreshing conversations
Make the surrounding air fresher

Like the dewdrops hanging on a fully bloomed morning glory
Love notes hang on the music paper
So that happiness makes more cords

This is a happy meal, and
It is better because it is with you

행복한 밥상

커튼이 걷히자
강·된장이 올라선 호박잎쌈에
싸여있는 구수한 잡곡밥이
나를 반긴다

쌈에서 무르익는
싱그러운 대화
주위의 공기를 더욱 상큼하게 만든다

활짝 핀 나팔꽃에 매달린 이슬처럼
오선지에 사랑의 음표가 매달려
더욱더 행복은 화음을 낸다

행복한 밥상인데
그대와 함께여서 더욱 좋다

Between seasons

I count the time
That dragged
My life thus far

While shaking off leaves and fruits
In the winter wind
I step on the fallen leaves scattered on the forest path.

Forgotten while being flitted by winds
Memories
When they are taken out, one by one
Sometimes in regret
Sometimes in joy
I reminisce the time that is reviving

The sound of the mountain wind
Brings me into a serene and clean calm
The sensitive reaction that has just been combed out

계절과 계절 사이

나의 삶을
지금까지 끌고 온
세월을 헤아려본다

겨울바람에 잎이랑 열매
훨훨 뿌리치며
숲길에 널브러진 가랑잎을 밟는다

바람에 스치며 잊고 있었던
추억들
하나씩 둘씩 끄집어내면
때로는 후회에
때로는 기쁨에
되살아나는 시간을 회상해 본다

산바람 소리
갓 빗어낸 예민한 반응을
차분하고 정결하게 가라앉힌다

After opening a path in the inner side without any distracting thoughts
Every time I take a step
My heart becomes audacious

아무 잡념 없는 내면에 여로를 열고
한 걸음 한 걸음 걸을 때마다
두둑해지는 나의 마음

Azalea

To shed tears due to the red passion
I cannot forget his name
Wherever you go
I would like to wish you comfort

Without any reason why, I cannot look up at the sky
Due to the longing that bloomed before the leaves
I came here following spring

Somehow by bowing my head
Not knowing
You who came all the way to beneath my chin
Since I miss you today too
I am blooming pink flowers

진달래

붉은 정열에 눈물겹도록
그분 이름만은 잊지 못한다
가는 곳 어디에서라도
편안함을 빌어주고 싶다

하늘 우러러보지 못할 이유 없이
잎보다 먼저 피어난 그리움에
봄 따라 여기까지 왔다

어이 고개 숙여
턱밑까지 찾아온 너를
내가 알지 못한 채
오늘도 보고 싶어
분홍빛 꽃을 피우고 있다

Grass Eliminator

At the sound of the grass eliminator
The green color of cutting dawn is refreshing.

Without neglecting given tasks
The grass eliminator works
It is fresh and boastful

Wildflowers that whisper the secrets of nature
And even the insects that stayed on the roadside wake up in surprise.
In despair
They look at the grass eliminator with sad faces

예초기

예초기 소리에
새벽이 잘리는 초록빛이 함초롬하다

맡은 일 소홀함 없이
일하는 예초기
싱그럽고 자랑스럽다

자연의 비밀을 속삭이는 들꽃과
길가에 머물던 벌레들도 놀라 일어나
낙담 속
슬픈 얼굴로 예초기를 바라본다

Locust Rice

Blessed land
Golden field
Where clear water and clean air
And natural climatic conditions are in harmony

A sunny spring day
The pregnancy that sprouted as droplets between the leaves
Grows new life

After avoiding pests and diseases, and
Enduring typhoons and the moonlight that leads to sleep
After passing the season of suffering came the maturity to bow the head

When the long journey ended
Beyond the nervousness of waiting
An ear of rice is born as a grain
It is a precious gift that came riding on the autumn wind.

메뚜기 쌀

맑은 물과 깨끗한 공기
천혜의 기후조건이 어우러진
복받은 땅
황금 들녘

봄볕 따사롭던 날
잎새 사이 방울방울 움 틔운 잉태
새 생명을 키워간다

병충해를 피해 가고
태풍에 잠재우는 달빛에
인고의 계절 지나 고개 숙인 성숙

긴 여정이 끝나면
기다림 속 초조함을 넘어서서
알곡으로 탄생한 한 톨의 벼 이삭
가을바람 타고 온 소중한 선물이다

Sitting on the shoulder, the scarecrow
Wearing a straw hat
Sparrows' song is cheerful.

Between the ears of rice
Locusts jump and nature breathes
Plump locust rice is
Full of happiness

밀짚모자 눌러쓴
허수아비 어깨 위 앉아 있는
참새들의 노래가 흥에 겹다

벼 이삭 사이
메뚜기가 뛰고 자연이 살아 숨 쉬는
토실토실한 메뚜기 쌀에
행복이 가득하다

Chapter 2
Comma of Summer

제2장
여름의 쉼표

Comma of Summer

A hot and hard asphalt road and
A leisurely country road
Are in contrast with each other

In the countryside, the sound of unknown grass bugs.
Open the road leisurely, and
Even birds walk as companions.

The footsteps with a crunch speak of the texture of the soil.
At the scent of roses blooming in hot summer
I draw a comma for a while

Under the cool shade provided by the trees
Hidden pleasure
Steps on a country road are leisurely.

여름의 쉼표

뜨겁고 딱딱한 아스팔트 길과
유유자적한 시골길이
대조가 된다

시골에는 알 수 없는 풀벌레 소리
한가롭게 길을 열고
새들도 길동무 삼아 걸음을 옮긴다

사박사박 발걸음은 흙의 질감을 말하고
뜨거운 여름에 피어나는 장미 향기에
잠깐 쉼표를 그려 본다

나무가 내어 주는 시원한 그늘에
숨겨진 즐거움
시골길 걸음이 여유롭다

Forest park

In Hamyang where
Sunlight is hidden in refreshing rain streaks
Warm rain is falling

In a forest full of dense trees
With forest bathing
I breathe the mystery of nature

In the quiet rain
Felt after closing eyes like a girl
Beautiful wild flowers bloom

Poppy flowers that dyed the field red before I know
Flower buds holding drizzle
The smell of a woman's shampoo is moist.

I am drawing trees with a picture, and
The precious mysteries of nature
With a sculpture

삼림공원

청량한 빗줄기에 햇빛을 감춘
함양에
따스한 비가 내린다

울창한 나무들이 빼곡한 나무 숲속
삼림욕으로
자연의 신비를 호흡한다

소녀처럼 눈감고 느껴보는
고요한 비에
아름다운 들꽃이 핀다

어느새 들판을 붉게 물들인 양귀비꽃
이슬비 머금은 꽃봉오리
여인의 샴푸 냄새가 촉촉하다

그림으로 나무를 그리고
조각으로
자연의 소중한 신비를 그려내고 있다

Husband

A strange degree of kinship, which is neither father nor brother
A person who is both close and distant
With whom I discuss closely sometimes
And I cannot talk other times

Sometimes hurts me to the extent to be thought to be an enemy.
But sometimes can easily say that he loves me the most
The man

As time goes by
The person who even taught me war

A wildly strange person
Who is hateful sometimes, but becomes favorite other times
A strange person
With whom I cook dinner, and eat together today too.

남편

아빠도 아니고 오빠도 아닌 이상한 촌수
어떨 땐 가깝게 의논하다가
말할 수 없는
가깝고도 먼 사람

원수인가 싶도록 마음 상하다가
가장 사랑한다고 쉽게 말할 수 있는
남자

시간이 흐를수록
나에게 전쟁까지 가르쳐 주는 사람

싫다가도 좋아지는
걷잡을 수 없이 묘한 사람
오늘도 저녁을 지어서 함께 먹는
이상한 사람

Hydrangea

Drunk with an ecstatic and fragrant purple
I meditate silently in the front yard of Daeungjeon Hall

Are your favorite flowers
White? Or purple?
I search the flowers with anxiety

Flowers appearing in multiple colors
What is their karma of the previous life
That makes them bloom beautifully in many colors

I miss my childhood
The old days
When I was innocent and pretty; not knowing the path of asceticism

수국

황홀하고 향긋한 보랏빛에 취하여
대웅전 앞뜰에서 묵언수행을 한다

그대 좋아하는 꽃은
흰색일까? 보라색일까?
가슴 조이며 꽃을 찾는다

여러 색깔로 나타나는 꽃
전생의 업이 어떠하기에
여러 색깔로 아름답게 피어날까

지난날
고행의 길도 모르던 천진난만 하고 예뻤던
어린 시절이 그립다

Hail

Probably angry at something, the summer sky
Is vomiting showers and pieces of ice

Pieces of ice clear like crystal
Fall as a hail larger than coins
To make farmers feel heartsore

Sound of pouring like roasting beans
Ice grains vomited for quite a while
Make farmers worry about the agricultural products they have cultivated thus far.

Looking at the bruised and perforated holes in each leaf of crops
The sighs the farmers spit out are bitter

우박

여름 하늘은 무엇 땜에 화가 났는지
소나기와 얼음조각을 토해내고 있다

수정처럼 맑은 얼음조각
동전보다 큰 우박으로 떨어져
농심을 아리게 한다

콩 볶 듯 쏟아내는 소리
한바탕 토해낸 얼음 알갱이
여태껏 지어놓은 농산물을 걱정하게 된다

농작물의 잎마다 피멍과 뚫린 구멍을 보며
내뱉는 농민의 한숨 소리가 씁쓸하다

Old Newspaper

Holding a newspaper of yesterday
To know today
Is a foolish thing

Because there is no present
Although the future may be predicted
From the past life

If you stick to and are hurt by the past
Only lament will be alive
And only time will laugh at us
No matter how hard a life or no matter how abundant a life you have lived,
Isn't the past just the past?

Although yesterday was difficult
And an exhausting road
I will live with a will filled with hope for tomorrow

지난 신문

하루가 지나 버린 신문을 들고
오늘을 알려는 것은
어리석은 일

지나간 삶에서
미래를 예측할지 모르지만
현재가 없기 때문이다

과거에 집착하고 아파하면
한탄만 살아있어
시간이 우릴 비웃을 뿐
아무리 힘겹고 풍족한 삶을 살았어도
과거는 과거가 아닌가

어제가 힘겨웠고
고단한 길이었어도
내일을 위해 희망찬 의지로 살아가련다

Moonlight Love

In the lake
At the moonlight that knocks my heart
Your beautiful appearance glimmers

Glowing like flames
My heart
Wants to penetrate into you

When your lovely voice
Stays in the rim of my ear as the harsh moonlight breathes
It becomes a still harsher breath
And fills up my heart

Round moon hanging at the tip of a green branch
Ripening under it
Longing is pathetic

달빛 사랑

호수 속
내 가슴을 두드리는 달빛에
그대 아름다운 모습이 아른댄다

불꽃처럼 피어나는
이 마음
그대 안에 스며들고 싶다

그대 고운 음성
혹독한 달빛의 숨결로
귓전에 머물면
거친 숨결 되어
내 가슴을 가득 채운다

푸른 나뭇가지 끝에 걸린 둥근 달
그 아래 영글어 가는
그리움이 애처롭다

If I become your beautiful flower
I would like to make you drunk with the fragrance of love
Fall asleep on my petals

Our relationship
I would like to weave finely
To make moonlight love

내가 그대의 아름다운 꽃이 되면
그댄 사랑의 향기에 취해
나의 꽃잎에 잠들게 하고 싶다

우리의 인연을
곱게 엮어
달빛 사랑을 하고 싶다

Summer Rain

Raindrops
Wake up the sleeping grass

Clovers that became pale due to broiling sunshine
May be immersed in some thought
Are bowing their heads

Like grass leaves wet with rain
My heart wet with longing
Blooms flowers gently in the grass

여름비

빗방울이
잠든 풀잎을 깨운다

뙤약볕에 핼쑥해진 토끼풀
무슨 생각에 잠긴 건지
머리를 숙이고 있다

비에 젖은 풀잎처럼
그리움에 젖은 내 마음
풀밭에서 사르르 꽃을 피운다

Wild Rose

Without being colored in green in the forest
White flowers bloom in starlight

When the morning comes
Wake up early
To exchange greetings with a smile

Even if wanton to warmly open arms
And hugs
It is not easily permitted because there are small thorns

Wild roses that bloom and fall
Because they like the hearts of mountains
And the scent of pine
I would like to become a white wild rose

찔레꽃

숲속 푸르름에 물들지 않고
별빛 속에서 피어나는 하얀 꽃

아침이 되면
일찍 깨어나
미소로 인사를 나눈다

따뜻이 두 팔 벌려
껴안아 주고 싶어도
작은 가시가 있어 쉽게 허락하지 않는다

산속이 좋고
솔향이 좋아
피고 지는 하얀 찔레꽃
나는 하얀 찔레꽃이 되고 싶다

Greeting June

Among the twelve months of the year
That will be met inevitably
June came

On the corner of the road through which the heat comes
The perfume of verdure that approaches freshly
At the foot of the mountain where green leaves sway
Baby birds play music

In the feast of blessing in a dense forest
When the daytime moon ripens further
With the excitement that blooms in the fragrance of fascination
They greet roses

유월을 맞으며

일 년 열두 달 가운데
필연적으로 만날
6월이 왔다

더위가 오는 길목에서
싱그럽게 다가오는 신록의 향수
초록 이파리가 일렁이는 산기슭에서
아기 새들이 연주를 한다

녹음 짙은 축복의 향연 속
낮달이 한결 영글어 가면
매혹의 향기에 피어나는 설렘으로
장미꽃을 맞고 있다

The Rainy Season

Tap dance that taps the roof of the farmer's hut
I hope the steps will flow along the waterway now.

Sitting on a plastic chair
When I look out
Trees standing in the mountains
Look clean like a baby who just finished a bath

When the sparrows that were singing while sitting on the railing
Take a deep sleep
It's hard to listen to the beautiful songs

The scent of coffee flows in a pretty glass
The memories that were kept in my heart
Are revived

The rainfalls become a waterfall
And are busy to go their way
Longing also becomes like river water, and flows over time

장마

농막 지붕을 두드리는 탭 댄스
이제그만 발길도 물길 따라 흐르면 좋겠다

플라스틱 의자에 걸터앉아
밖을 내다보면
산야에 서 있는 나무들
갓 목욕을 끝낸 아기같이 깨끗하다

난간에 앉아 노래하던 참새들이
깊은 잠을 자면
아름다운 노래 소리 듣기가 힘든다

예쁜 잔에 커피 향기가 흘러나오고
내 마음속에 간직했던 추억도
되살아난다

장맛비가 폭포 되어
제 갈 길 가기에 바쁘고
그리움도 시간 따라 강물 되어 흐른다

Handwritten Letter

Hand written letters written with heart
Are contained on paper

In every phrase that flutters in the wind
I struggle to insert even a whispering voice

The heart of the loved one
Like white snow, letters are piled up in a heap

In the river flowing through the heart, in which jade waves are rolling
A feeling of happiness is dissolved

When life, like sweet cotton candy,
Is painted over with longing
A rainbow appears in the handwritten letter

손 편지

마음을 담아 쓴 손 글씨
종이 위에 담는다

바람에 나부끼는 구절마다
속삭이는 목소리까지 끼워 넣으려 애쓴다

사랑하는 이에게 보내는 마음
흰 눈처럼 글자가 소복이 쌓인다

옥빛 물결 출렁이는 마음속 흐르는 강물에
행복감을 풀어 넣는다

달콤한 솜사탕 같은 삶에
그리움을 덧칠하면
손 편지에 무지개가 뜬다

First Love

A fantasy of reminiscences full of scents
A person who passed by me
So that I want to keep it forever
As sweet, unrequited love
It was a deeply fragrant first love

Even though as time passed the annual rings grew bigger
Always left with longing
The body odor

In the regret of a novice who could not fulfill his first love
Without anyone knowing
Heartsore is felt

첫사랑

향기 가득한 추억의 몽환
달콤한 짝사랑으로
고이 간직하고 싶도록
내 곁을 스쳐 간 사람
향내 짙은 첫사랑이었다

세월이 흘러 나이테가 커져도
언제나 그리움으로 남아있는
체취

첫사랑은 못다 한 풋내기의 미련에
아무도 모르게
가슴 아린다

Leisurely Early Summer

Spring was nice because it was spring, but
These days added with heat
Are filled with a fine scent

Although always busy and things that must be done are overflowing
When the roses over the fence smile
The scent of acacia flowers is delicate

Lettuce and crown daisy that grow well verdantly
All kinds of abundance
Come into my eyes

In a state of nature
The sun-drenched streets are getting hotter
There are cold winters too

What beautiful seasons
Even for my mind and body that get tired easily,
I look for a place to rest leisurely

여유로운 초여름

봄은 봄이라서 좋았지만
더위까지 겹친 요즘
고운 향기로 채워진다

늘 바빠할 일이 넘쳐나지만
담장 너머엔 장미가 웃으면
아카시아 꽃향기가 은은하다

파릇파릇 잘 자라는 상추와 쑥갓
온갖 풍성함이
눈에 들어온다

자연 그대로
햇살 내려앉은 거리가 더워지고
차가운 겨울도 있다

참으로 아름다운 계절들
쉬이 지치는 정신과 몸에도
여유롭게 쉬어 갈 쉼터를 찾는다

July 7th in the Lunar Calendar

Struggling with longing
Magpie's sound
Is a promise to meet on July 7th.

Resolving ardent longing to the bone
It sounds like a precious cry

The rain that fell in the evening
Are tears of joy
That flowed down from Ojakgyo Bridge

If it rains at dawn of the next day
It may be the tears of farewell shed
Because the Milky Way cannot be crossed

Trembling with regret at the end of the season
Since the hand holding the skirt cannot be released
Even the wind is sad

칠월칠석

그리움에 몸부림치는
까치 소리
칠월칠석에 만나자는 약속이다

애틋한 사무침을 푸는
소중한 외침으로 들린다

저녁에 내린 비는
오작교에서 흘러내린
기쁨의 눈물

다음 날 새벽에 비가 내리면
은하수 건너지 못해
흘리는 이별의 눈물이려나

계절의 끝자락에서 아쉬움에 떨며
치마 부여잡은 손 놓지 못해
바람까지 슬프구나

Dandelion

Small dandelions blooming on the new road
Due to a dislike of loneliness

With yellow
And white, no matter how much they show off
At some point, they fly up into the sky as spores.

Even the slender flapping of the wings of a dragonfly is not funny, and
The pollen carried by bees
Is boredom.
Loneliness is piling up day by day

Between the hard cement roads
Barely attaching its feet
A dandelion flower
Bears a sad smile

민들레

외로움이 싫어서
신작로 길에 피어있는 작은 민들레

노란색
하얀색으로 아무리 자신을 뽐내어도
어느 순간 홀씨로 훨훨 하늘로 날아오른다

잠자리의 가녀린 날갯짓도 우습지 않고
꿀벌이 날라다 주는 꽃가루도
싫증이 나고
외로움만 하루하루 쌓여간다

딱딱한 시멘트길 사이에
겨우 발을 붙인 채
민들레꽃 한 송이
슬픈 미소 머금었구나

A Sea That Is Embracing Secrets

A fist-sized stone was thrown into the sea.
The sea water is spattered and comes up to land.

Complaints were thrown into the sea
On the fishing rod that was used to stop the passage of time
Drenching longing
Comes up hanging dingle-dangle.

Running instinctively across a vast field
Waves surging like wild horses
For things that have not been acknowledged
To the extent that the uvula swells, the waves
Let out a yell

From the appearance and retirement of masked actors
The sea knows the truth

비밀을 품은 바다

주먹만 한 돌을 바다에 던졌다
바닷물이 튕겨 뭍으로 올라온다

푸념을 바다에 던졌다
세월을 막으려 했던 낚싯대에
그리움이 흥건하게
대롱대롱 매달려 올라온다

광활한 들판을 본능적으로 질주하는
야생마같이 밀려오는 파도
인정받지 못한 일들에
파도는 목젖이 붓도록
고함을 지른다

가면을 쓴 배우들의 등장과 은퇴까지
바다는 진실을 알고 있다

Being at the full term
The sea that cannot but wait for the stars until the night falls
Even if I tell secrets and forget them when I turn around
I come to go to the sea again

만삭이 되어
밤이 되도록 별을 기다릴 수밖에 없는 바다
비밀을 털어놓고 돌아서면 잊어버려도
나는 바다를 다시 찾게 된다

Chapter 3
When Hungry for Life

제3장
삶에 허기질 때

When Hungry for Life

I miss love
That will make each other's heart clear
Like a deer with clear eyes

When hungry for life
Coming to mind at beautiful moments
The names that were precious
Calling out one by one
I look back upon the passion that was hot like blood

Waiting for a future that has not yet come true
My appearance
Drawing once again
I have courage to take care of tomorrow

삶에 허기질 때

눈이 맑은 사슴처럼
서로의 가슴을 맑게 해줄
사랑이 그립다

삶에 허기질 때
아름답던 순간에 떠오르는
소중했던 이름들
하나씩 불러보며
피처럼 뜨거웠던 열정을
돌이켜 본다

아직 이루어지지 않은 미래를 기다리는
나의 모습을
다시 한번 그려가며
용기 내어 내일을 가꾸어 본다

Companion

The fluttering that enters my red heart
Is it curiosity?
Attraction?
Or, love?

In a small teacup, I
Put a small world.

With a pure white dream
If I unfold my dream of a sweet life with you
You should be my companion

동반자

붉은 심장 속으로 들어오는 설렘
호기심일까?
끌림일까?
아님, 사랑일까?

나는 작은 찻잔에
올망졸망한 세상을 채워 본다

새하얀 꿈을 안고
달콤한 삶의 꿈을 너와 함께 펼쳐보면
너는 나의 동반자이어라

Coffee and Music

When I am in agony concentrating on life
I like to open up my heart
A cup of coffee becomes a temporary bridge of each other
My heart becomes soft
The flowing music also strokes the soul, and
Makes me take more courage

Not only by being inseparable
Small celebration of joy
But also by the sadness that deepens due to loneliness, being consoled
Into my heart dancing lively with excitement
The scent of coffee seeps

An elegant feeling with the bitter taste of coffee
Became my daily life

During high school days with short hair
At a music cafe
I could not but be fascinated by the beautiful melody.

커피와 음악

삶에 집중하며 고뇌할 때
마음이라도 터놓고 싶다
커피 한 잔은 서로의 가교가 되어
마음이 부드러워지고
흐르는 음악도 영혼을 어루만지며
나에게 용기를 더하게 한다

떼어놓을 수 없는
작은 기쁨의 축하뿐 아니라
외로움에 짙어지는 슬픔에도 위로를 받으며
흥겨움에 덩실대는 마음에
커피 향내가 스민다

커피의 쓴맛에 우아한 느낌이
나의 일상이 되었다

단발머리 여고 시절
음악다방에서

The song of a singer
Still rings in my ears
I just miss those times

When the month of May - when the green leaves deepen
- has come
I place a cup of espresso coffee in front of me
I watch Vivaldi's Waltz, and
Look out the window

아름다운 선율에 매혹되지 않을 수 없던
어느 가수의 노래가
아직 귓가를 맴돌아
그때가 그립기만 하다

신록에 짙어가는 오월이 되면
나는 에스프레소 커피 한 잔을 앞에 두고
비발디의 왈츠를 감상하며
창밖으로 시선을 옮긴다

Meeting in Anticipation

Holding an armful of longing
Wandering the rainy streets without an umbrella
I set out on a journey to find happiness

Because of my longing for him
When I walk alone on the street
I feel a thrill of joy throughout my body.

Some day in the future
Looking at each other
With eyes of trust and understanding
We will embrace each other with a warm heart

With respect and generosity rather than possessions
He will embrace me in a coat with a raised collar
I would like to walk with him with a bright smile

기대 속의 만남

보고픔을 한아름 안고
우산 없이 비 내리는 거리를 서성이며
행복 찾아 길을 나선다

그의 모습 보고픔에
혼자 길을 거니면
나의 전신에 기쁨의 전율을 느낀다

후일에 언젠가
서로를 쳐다보며
신뢰와 이해의 눈으로
따뜻한 마음으로 보듬게 되겠지

소유보다 존경과 아낌으로
깃을 세운 코트에 나를 감싸 안아줄
그이와 함께 정갈한 웃음으로 걷고 싶다

Sauce of Love

Salad is delicious
Because apples, lettuce, and vegetables
Are mixed with a sauce.

In our life too
Me 50%
You 50%
When the two are added up to 100%
The sauce of faith and trust to understand each other are mixed
So that delicious and fragrant love is born

사랑의 소스

샐러드가 맛있는 것은
사과, 양상추, 야채에
소스를 버무리기 때문이다

우리의 삶에도
나 50%
그대 50%
둘이 합해서 100% 되면
서로를 이해하는 믿음과 신뢰의 소스를 버무려
맛있고 향기로운 사랑이 탄생 된다

When I Have Been to an Alumni Meeting

Midday when summer pours
The chattering sound is hot.

Although appearances have changed a lot
The hearts are as they were when they were young
Friends who are precious to me
Yesterday's moments unfold as landscapes

Before saying, "hello"
Longing mingles with the time that has passed
To deeply dye my heart.

동창회 다녀와서

여름이 쏟아지는 한낮
재잘대는 소리가 뜨겁다

외모는 많이 변했어도
마음은 어릴 때 모습을 지닌
나에게는 소중한 친구들
어제의 순간들이 풍경으로 펼쳐진다

안부를 묻기 전
흘러간 시간에 그리움이 어우러져
내 마음을 짙게 물들이고 있다

Pumpkin Flower

After a long time of waiting
Sticking out orange lips
You came deep into my heart

You open your comely and dainty mouth
With a fragrant language
To shake my heart

Having rosy passion
With a face smiling brightly
Pumpkin is ripening

Because you are full of confidence?
Or you are generous?
In response to the complaint, "Are pumpkin flowers also flowers?"
Without even blinking an eye
You smile waiting for your loved one

호박꽃

오래 기다린 세월
주황색 입술 내밀며
마음 깊게 다가온 너

곱살스럽고 앙증맞은 입을 열어
향기 짙은 언어로
내 마음을 흔들고 있구나

장밋빛 정열을 가진 채
활짝 웃는 얼굴로
영글어 가는 호박

자신감이 충만해서일까?
마음이 넓어서일까?
"호박꽃도 꽃이냐"는 투정에
눈 하나 꿈쩍 않고
사랑하는 이 기다리며 웃음 짓는 너

Even when the passing wind slightly winks
Without even looking at it
You greet the sunlight and embrace me

지나가는 바람이 슬쩍 윙크해도
보지도 않고
햇살을 맞이하고 나를 품는구나

Water Lily Blooming on the Lakeside

A pretty color, and straight and long, well-proportioned figure
You have got envy in your body

Slender stature and swaying gestures even in a gentle wind
You, who retain beauty even if you live only one day
Your name is pretty, and the flower is beautiful too.

The steps of many people who walk to and from the small lake
Even though it is a journey to live with quick steps
Love blooms

Time reflected in the lapping waves
A pretty water lily is even more precious.

호숫가에 핀 수련

고운 빛깔에 쭉쭉 뻗은 팔등신
부러움을 한 몸에 품었구나

늘씬한 키에 부드러운 바람에도 살랑대는 몸짓
하루를 살아도 예쁨을 간직한 너
이름도 예쁘고 꽃도 아름답구나

작은 호수에 오가는 많은 사람들의 발걸음
잰걸음으로 살아가는 여정이라도
피어나는 사랑

찰랑거리는 물결에 비춰오는 세월
예쁜 수련이 더욱 귀 하구나

Flu

The gaping hole through which
The fish caught in the net escape slowly
Is like a tunnel where an accident occurred.

Due to the rain falling all day
The mountain collapsed and the water overflowed
Like a runny nose with the flu.

When I take medicine, my head spins,
And there is an effect to make the eyes sleep, but
Judgments are clouded

Before getting wet with the monsoon rain
I should take some medicine
To get over the flu

Someday, after time passes,
The farmer dreams of the day when he will recover again, but
He gave up on everything

His body becomes heavy, and
He is exhausted

독감

그물에 걸린 고기들이
슬금슬금 빠져나가는 터진 구멍은
사고 난 터널 같다

온종일 내리는 비에
산이 무너지고 물이 넘쳐
독감 걸린 콧물 같다

약을 먹으면 머리가 빙글빙글 돌고
눈에 잠이 오는 효과는 있지만
판단이 흐릿해진다

장맛비에 몸이 젖기 전
약이라도 먹어
독감을 이겨내야 한다

언젠가 시간이 흐르고 나면
다시 회복될 날을 꿈꿔 보지만
모든 것을 체념한 농부

몸이 무거워지고
기운이 다 빠진다

Lotus Flower

Covers the world fully

Pink leaves, clean energy
When the wind passes
The gentle scent of flowers rides the wind blowing over the water
To seep into my breath.

Although it was known to bloom in the pond
The beautiful flower blooms in my heart too

Endlessly, and
Quietly, purifies the world

연꽃

세상을 가득 담는다

분홍빛 잎새 정결한 기운
바람이 지날 때면
은은한 꽃향기 물바람 타고
내 숨결에 스며든다

연못에 피는 줄 알았지만
내 마음에도 피어나는 아름다운 꽃

세상을 끝없이
고요히 정화하고 있다

West Wind in the Alley

Due to the raging wind
Clawing at the valley
Fire cannot be set in the furnace.

The wind, in its way,
Is busy to go its way, and
My mind is busy too, as a fire should be set.

There is nothing
That I can handle as I please
Only bearing and enduring
Seem to be right.

When the mind and fingertips achieve serenity
The wind blowing to the farm hut
Begins to tranquilize

골목의 하늬바람

골짜기를 할퀴며
휘몰아치는 바람에
아궁이에 불을 지필 수 없다

바람은 바람대로
제 갈 길에 바쁘고
불을 붙여야 될 마음도 바쁘기만 하다

내 마음대로 다룰 수 있는 것이
하나도 없다
참고 견디는 것만이
옳을 것 같다

마음과 손끝이 평정을 이룰 때
농막으로 불어대는 바람은
잠잠해지기 시작한다

Contemplation on a Rainy Day

Raindrops falling on a tin roof
The sound of the piano is loud for a spell.

The waterway that dances at the end of the angled rafter
Is a masterpiece created in harmony
Like the figure of the baby of Dionysus.

Accepting the wine made by the soil as my friend
I settle my mind for a while, and
Start a new life

With a cup of coffee that sheds a strong aroma on a simple table
When I enjoy the scenery of distant mountains
I find it is more beautiful than a watercolor painting

In a shaggy countryside buried in nature
When it rains
I am absorbed into the precious scenery of a small bit of happiness.

비 오는 날의 사색

양철 지붕에 내리는 빗방울
한바탕 피아노 소리가 요란하다

추녀 끝에 춤추는 물길은
디오니소스의 아기 모습과 같이
어우러져 빚어내는 명작이다

흙이 빚어낸 포도주를 벗 삼아
잠시 마음을 가다듬고
새로운 삶을 시작한다

소박한 탁자에 짙게 풍기는 커피로
먼 산의 풍경을 즐기면
한 폭의 수채화보다 더 아름답다

자연에 묻힌 텁수룩한 시골
비 내리는 날이 되면
소소한 행복의 값진 풍경에 빠져든다

Hiking in the Rain

It rains
Trees soaked with water.

From yellowish green
Into fresh green turned the oak tree
The tips of the branches stretch up with moisture.

One raindrop
Falls on my heart

New strength rises in the raindrops that have been drizzling
With the song of the birds in the mountains or
The scent of flowers
My garden is filled up

At Seunghaksan Mountain
Still
The welcomed sound of falling rain is heard

우중 산행

비가 온다
수목들에 물기가 배었다

연둣빛에서
싱싱한 초록으로 바뀐 참나무
가지 끝이 촉촉이 뻗어 오른다

빗방울 하나
내 마음에 떨어진다

부슬대던 빗방울에 새 힘이 솟고
산속의 새들의 노래나
꽃들의 향기로
나의 정원을 가득히 채운다

승학산에는
아직도
단비 내리는 소리가 들린다

Night When Violets Bloom

In the sunny garden
The sound of purple violet petals opening
Longing opens memories

In the purple petals
Gray memories seeped
As the night is deep
I fall asleep to the sound of blooming violets

제비꽃 피는 밤

햇살 따사로운 정원에
보랏빛 제비꽃잎 열리는 소리
그리움이 추억을 연다

보랏빛 꽃잎 속에
스며든 회색의 추억들
밤은 깊어
제비꽃 피는 소리에 잠이 든다

Sad Dandelion

Alone
On a rough roadside
A shabby dandelion standing in tears

Due to the dust sprinkled by passing cars
No matter how pretty it decorates
Only futile desires are rolling around

The face washed with morning dew
No time to dry in the sun
Despair overtakes it again
The world becomes hateful

Even if it gets stuck between stones and cannot grow,
If there was a chance to live cleanly
It could look up at the pretty sky smiling...

The dandelions are sad

슬픈 민들레

홀로
거친 길섶에서
눈물지며 서 있는 남루한 민들레

지나가는 자동차가 뿌리는 먼지에
아무리 예쁘게 단장해도
허무한 욕망만 뒹굴고 있다

아침 이슬로 씻은 얼굴
햇볕에 말릴 틈 없이
또다시 덮어쓰는 절망감
세상이 싫어진다

차라리 돌 틈 사이 끼어 자라지 못한다 해도
깨끗하게 살 수 있는 기회가 있다면
미소 지으며 예쁜 하늘을 쳐다볼 수 있을 텐데...

민들레는 슬프다

Toward the Blooming of Lotus Petals

No matter how much they roll over the large leaves,
They look untainted
I would like to resemble them

On the lips of Buddha with a benevolent smile,
The sound of silent laughter is majestic

Unable to let go of love
My pink heart
He is still watching allusively

연꽃잎 필 무렵

커다란 잎 위에 아무리 뒹굴어도
때 묻지 않는 모습
닮고 싶다

인자한 미소 짓는 부처님 입술에는
무언의 웃음소리가 장엄하다

사랑을 놓지 못한
핑크빛 내 마음
지금도 넌지시 보고 있구나

Ginkgo Nut

The old tree, the guardian deity of my hometown,
Is holding tens of thousands of fruits like fate
In autumn that bowed its head

Jewels that fell because they couldn't endure anymore
Give out a terrible smell
Then, the steps of the Pierrot wearing boots are heavy.

Transparent and moist, jaded and beady ginkgo nuts
If placed on white boiled rice
It becomes a healthy meal with soft meat.

Ginkgo nuts are transformed into a blood circulation agent
To comfort the hearts of the sick
Thereby making them sing with joy

은행

고향의 수호신인 고목이
수만 개의 열매를 운명처럼 달고 있는
고개 숙인 가을

참다못해 맥없이 낙하한 보석들
지독한 냄새를 풍기면
장화 신은 피에로의 발길이 무겁다

투명하고 촉촉한 옥구슬 은행알들
하얀 쌀밥 위에 얹으면
육질 부드러운 건강밥상이 된다

혈액순환제로 변신하여
아픈 자의 마음을 위로하여
기쁨으로 노래를 부르게 한다

Chapter 4
Four-o'clock, My Elder Sister

제4장
분꽃 언니

Four-o'clock, My Elder Sister

Precious and beautiful
My elder sister
The more I think about her, the more my heart aches.

When she saw the flowers, she thought it was spring and smiled.
On a lonely road where white snow falls
At the sight of her walking white
I was sad in the winter, I remember

A path we will walk together throughout our lives
She promised
I can't find it now
Only loneliness remains

Due to my heart desperately wanting to see her
With my ardent longing
I wet my eyes

분꽃 언니

소중하고 아름다운
나의 언니
생각할수록 가슴 저민다

꽃을 보면 봄인 줄 알고 웃음 지었고
흰 눈 내리는 외로운 길을
하얗게 걸어가던 뒷모습에
슬펐던 겨울이 생각난다

일생 함께 걸어갈 길
약속 해놓고
지금은 찾아볼 수 없는
쓸쓸함만 남아 있다

보고픈 마음 간절한
애틋한 그리움에
나의 눈시울을 적신다

Under the sunny wall
When spring comes and flowers bloom
I miss you blooming like a four-o'clock
My elder sister

양지바른 담벼락 아래
봄이 와 꽃이 피면
분꽃으로 피어나는 보고픈
나의 언니

Waves Surging upon the Beach

Even though my feet get wet by the surging waves
Rather than avoiding them, I am attracted by the coolness.
I try on the newly purchased aqua shoes

Even if I walk on fine sand brought in by the wind,
Without getting tired
The soles of my feet feel comfortable.
I taste the joy

When the can of beer I drank yesterday rises, and
Steps on the white waves
The dream swelling in one corner of my heart is dense.

Following the memories of the past
Surging like waves
I walk on the beach with a warm heart

해변에 밀려오는 파도

밀려온 파도에 발이 젖어도
피하기보다 시원함에 끌리는 마음
새로 구입한 아쿠아슈즈를 신어 본다

바람이 몰고 온 고운 모래밭을 걸어도
지치지 않고
발바닥이 편안을 느끼는
즐거움을 맛본다

어제 마시던 맥주가 떠올라
흰 파도를 밟으면
가슴 한편에 부풀어 오르는 꿈이 짙다

파도처럼 밀려오는
지난날의 추억을 따라
따뜻한 마음을 안고 해변을 걷는다

Starry Night

Starry night
The darkness gets darker, and
The strong wind takes away the fog

Beneath the silent mountain ridge
Thatched houses huddled together
The lights go out one by one

By the Milky Way
The stars hold, and are hand-in-hand
Busy dancing with Ganggangsullae
Starlight that came to my dark heart
Even if it is shaken by the wind
Whispers love to me

Wandering in a dream with the one I miss
I would like to weave starlight into strings
To play the harp of love

별빛 내리는 밤

별빛 내리는 밤
어둠이 갈수록 짙어지고
세찬 바람은 안개를 거둬들인다

적막한 산등성이 아래
옹기종기 모여 있는 초가집들
하나씩 차례로 불이 꺼진다

은하수 가에서
별들은 서로 손을 잡고
강강술래로 춤을 추기에 바쁘다

캄캄했던 내 마음에 찾아온 별빛
바람에 흔들려도
나에게 사랑을 속삭인다

그리운 이와 함께 꿈속을 헤매며
별빛을 현으로 엮어
사랑의 하프를 연주하고 싶다

Hollyhock

Flowers bloomed together are more beautiful
Than flowers bloomed alone
Is because the flowers compete with each other to resemble each other.

While blooming and withering together
So that even death is not fearful
They find solace

The more they wither, the more they rely on each other.
People who live consoling each other
Endlessly in their hearts
Red and white hollyhocks bloom

접시꽃

홀로 핀 꽃보다 더 어울려 핀 꽃이
더욱 아름다운 것은
서로를 비교하며 닮아가기 때문이다

함께 피어나고 시들어 가면서
죽음조차 두렵지 않게
위안을 찾는다

시들수록 서로 의지하여
위로하며 살아가는 사람들
끝없이 마음속에
붉고 하얀 접시꽃이 핀다

Generous Heart

Not to determine unhappiness and happiness
With my judgment
I offer a prayer
In front of Sancheong Suseonsa temple

Rather than keeping my eyes tied to the ground
I want to have generous eyes
That can see far away

Although a cold heart
Makes even winter freeze
I pray to become a person
Who can melt others' painful suffering
With a gentle heart

So that I can become a wise and intelligent woman
With sincerity and faith
Who is a figure of a mother resembling a Buddha smile
And mercy does not leave my side
I hold my hands

넉넉한 가슴

내가 가진 판단으로 불행과 행복을
결정하지 않게 해달라고
산청 수선사 법당 앞에서
나는 기도를 올린다

시선을 땅에 묶어 두기보다
멀리 바라볼 수 있는
넉넉한 눈을 갖기를 원한다

차가운 가슴은
겨울도 얼어붙게 하지만
온화한 마음으로
남의 고통스런 아픔을 녹여내는
사람이 될 수 있도록 기도드린다

성실과 믿음에
현명하고 지혜로운 여자로
부처님 미소 닮은 어머니의 모습 되어
자비가 내 곁을 떠나지 않게
두 손 모은다

On an Autumn Day

In a faded season
Soothing
Light pink cosmos flower scent
Flutters thickly.

Always
In my journey
To calm the cold wind
It becomes silver grass to sing

Even if autumn wants to stay in its place
Passing by fluttering like a butterfly
White snow is falling all over the world

At the end of winter
When camellia flowers bloomed with the passion that is so white to be seen as red
Fall pitifully, one by one,
The news of spring coming is heard in the wind

가을날에

빛바랜 계절에
마음을 달래는
연분홍 코스모스 꽃향내가
짙게 출렁인다

언제나
나의 여정 속에서
차가운 바람을 잠재우려
억새 되어 노래하고 있다

가을이 제자리에 머물고 싶어도
나비처럼 한들거리며 지나가는
하얀 눈이 온 누리에 내리고 있다

겨울 끝자락에서
희다 못해 붉은 정열로 꽃피운 동백꽃이
애처롭게 한 송이씩 떨어지면
봄이 오는 소식이 바람결에 들린다

Dried Persimmon

When persimmon flowers that were smiling faintly
In the spring breeze
Carry the summer sun on their backs
Unripe and puckered persimmons are borne.

In the autumn wind
Persimmons that do not know that they are ripening
Are buried in the light of the round moon of Hangawi
And are embarrassed by the greenness that has been snorting
To become ripe persimmons.

In the north wind that came running at the first frost
Discouraged, dried persimmons with only passion remaining
Even the moisture was taken away from their entire body.

Left alone in the harsh winter
Wearing a crown bestowed by fruits
They become busy marching naked

곶감

봄바람에
배시시 웃던 감꽃
여름 태양 등에 업으면
땡감이 열린다

가을바람에
익어가는 줄 모르는 감
한가위 둥근 달빛에 묻혀
코웃음 치던 푸르름이 부끄러워
홍시가 된다

첫서리에 달려온 북풍에
정열만 남은 기죽은 곶감
온몸에 물기조차 빼앗겨 버렸다

엄동설한에 혼자 남아
과일들이 수여하는 왕관을 쓴 채
알몸으로 행진하기에 몹시 바빠진다

Ah,

To whom will we be sold?

The heart waiting today, and tomorrow too

Is full of anticipation rather than anxiety

아,
누구에게 팔려 갈까
오늘도 내일도 기다리는 마음
초조보다 기대로 가득하다

To My Son and Daughter

Baby
Mom and Dad
Are waiting for you with yearning

Under the clear sky
With overflowing love
To be with you
We dream of the future

In the world where people
Who boast of silver spoons
Or gold spoons, live

Just rapidly and healthily
Grow
Parents' mind wanting to give you a gold spoon
Is just desperation

아들과 딸에게

아가야
엄마 아빠는
너를 무척 기다린다

맑은 하늘 아래
넘치는 사랑으로
너와 함께할
미래를 꿈꾼다

은수저
금수저를 자랑하는
사람들이 사는 세상

무럭무럭 건강하게만
자라다오
너에게 금수저 주고 싶은 부모 마음
간절할 뿐이다

Dreaming of a time to meet you
We dream of a beautiful world

Baby

We love you
Let us meet each other healthy and strong

너와 만날 시간을 그리면서
아름다운 세상을 꿈꾼다

아가야

사랑한다
건강하고 튼튼하게 우리 서로 만나자

On the road with sea waves

Driven by the wind
The sound of the tide
Barely audible whispers by seashells
I listen to the story

Dogu Beach, where I was strolling amidst the five-colored lights
In the memories created by weaving solitude
Friends' stories of which nothing can be missed
Are high.

The teacup is getting colder.
At the sound of waves hitting my heart
Longing is rolling

Deep in the night
The fog is thick

해파랑길에서

바람에 밀려오는
밀물의 파도 소리
들릴 듯 말듯 조개들이 속삭이는
이야기를 듣는다

오색 불빛 속을 거닐던 도구 해변
고독을 엮어 만든 추억 속
하나도 빼놓을 수 없는
친구들의 이야기가 높다

찻잔은 점점 식어 가는데
가슴을 두드리는 파도 소리에
그리움이 출렁인다

깊은 밤에
안개가 짙다

Water Lily

Although no one is watching or interested
Water lilies with lots of conversations to share
Wander on the water until the sun sets on the western mountain.

On the muddy water
Sticking beautiful faces out
When I look at a water lily
My bad mind disappears completely

When my hesitant steps
Are looked back upon just once
So that I can maintain a beautiful appearance like a water lily
I would like to pray for beauty with both of my hands.

With cloudy mind
Although I hesitate for a long time
I live learning from you, who are sitting up straight on the water

수련

아무도 봐주거나 관심이 없어도
서로 나눌 대화가 많은 수련
해가 서산에 기울도록 물 위에서 서성인다

흙탕물 위에
아름다운 얼굴 내민
한 송이 수련을 보면
나의 나쁜 마음이 깨끗하게 사라진다

머뭇거리는 나의 발걸음
한번 뒤돌아보면
수련처럼 아름다운 자태를 간직할 수 있게
아름다움을 간절히 두 손 모아 빌고 싶다

흐린 마음
오래도록 머뭇거려도
물 위에 정좌한 너를 배우며 산다

Holding a Glass of Wine

Leaving behind the everyday life
That was extremely busy
Greenish gray-green grapes
I am reincarnated with Pinot Gris wine
Very sweet

The sound of crickets calling for fall
Is calling for autumn far away
Wine in my mouth
Has a fresh taste rich in tannin

My mouth filled with autumn
And a good scent
My heart gradually resembles the sky

와인 잔을 들며

혹독하게 바빴던
일상을 뒤로하고
푸른빛이 감도는 회색빛 청포도
피노그리PinotGris 포도주로 환생 되어
무척 감미롭다

가을을 재촉하는 귀뚜라미 소리
멀리 있는 가을을 부르고 있다
입 속 포도주
탄닌이 풍부하고 신선한 맛을 지닌다

가을이 가득해진 입 안
좋은 향기에
내 마음은 점점 하늘을 닮아간다

Night View

A dark night
When the moon quietly closes its eyes
As the frog chorus gets louder.
Starlight falls on submerged paddy fields

A village that sleeps soundly with the starlight as its lamp.
Occasionally a scops owl
Shakes the breeze
Everyone take a break
In the midnight when darkness thickly subsides
Eyelids unable to overcome sleepiness
Come down quietly

밤의 풍경

어둠이 짙게 내린 밤
달이 지그시 눈을 감을 때
개구리 합창 소리 높아지면.
별빛이 무논에 내린다

별빛을 등잔 삼아 단잠에 드는 마을
이따금 소쩍새가
산들바람을 흔든다

모두가 휴식을 취하고
캄캄한 어둠이 내려앉은 한밤
졸음에 못이긴 눈까풀
살그머니 내려온다

Forgotten Friend

A fresh friend
Who will be forgotten anyway as time passes

The youth, which was verdant
Due to a tangled mess of human relationships
Is like a withering leaf

Even in the hardships that were so deathly difficult,
My friend who seemed to be permanent

If she will be forgotten over time
I will let her flow into the river, in the rain
And not hold her

잊힌 친구

어차피 지나가면 잊힐
풋풋했던 친구

파릇파릇했던 청춘이
뒤죽박죽 얽혀버린 인간관계로
시들어가는 잎과 같다

죽을 만큼 힘들었던 고난에도
영원할 것 같던 나의 친구

시간이 지나면서 잊힐 것이라면
빗속에서 강물로 흘러버리고
붙들지 않으리라

Chisulryeong Mountain

A mountain not hateful no matter when I see
My heart sitting on the ridge
Is peaceful and enjoyable

Washed cleanly by the rain
The ice-melted stream
Is dazzling with ripples
Glittering in the sunlight between bush clovers

A heart that is empty of even echoes
Is surging in me with a calm joy

A pleasant mountain
That can be looked upon with a mind at ease.

With the moonlight hanging on the oak tree as my friend,
When a scops owl cries
The court in me is exposed to a clear wind.
Reading time
The poet's heart begins to revive

치술령 산

언제 봐도 싫지 않은 산
산마루에 걸터앉은 마음은
평화롭고 즐겁다

비에 말끔히 씻긴
얼음 녹은 시냇물은
사리 나무 사이에 햇살을 받아 일렁이는
잔물결에 눈이 부시다

메아리조차 비워버린 마음
내 안에서 잔잔한 기쁨으로 샘솟는다

마음 놓고 바라볼 수 있는
즐거운 산

굴참나무에 걸린 달빛을 벗 삼아
소쩍새 울어 대면
내 안의 뜰은 맑은 바람 쇠이며
세월을 읽는
시인의 마음이 소생하기 시작한다

Baby Swallow

Swallows that have made a home in a nest under the eaves
The chicks that have started chirping and flying are pretty.

Probably because they lived together with us under the same roof,
The baby swallows are without wariness
When I see them
Fighting over reasons and justifications
Humans are feeling ashamed

The lack of the aesthetics; of symbiosis and living in harmony is felt

새끼 제비

처마 밑 둥지에 가정을 차린 제비
짹짹거리며 날기 시작한 새끼들이 예쁘다

한 지붕 밑에서 함께 살아온 탓인지
경계심도 없는
귀여운 새끼 제비를 보면
이유와 명분에 아웅다웅하는
인간의 모습이 부끄럽게 느껴진다

어우러져 사는 공생의 미학이 아쉽다

On the Parents' Day

With no time to heal their sick bodies
My parents who sacrificed their entire lives
To raise six children

Immature youngest daughter
Who couldn't treat her mother well when she was alive.
And sent her a long way

When I look now, in my own maturity
My mother is not by my side
I am just heart-rending

When I attached a red carnation to her chest,
My mother
Quietly hugged me with a faint smile.

No matter how many carnations I put in front of her grave,
My heart becomes infinitely sad
Only my mother's face rises like a mist
I can't see clearly

어버이날에

아픈 몸 치료할 사이 없이
육 남매 키우시느라
일생 동안 희생하신 부모님

어머니 살아생전 잘해드리지 못하고
먼 길 보낸
철없는 막내딸

지금 겨우 철 들어 살펴보면
옆에 없는 어머니
내 가슴은 먹먹해질 뿐이다

빠알간 카네이션 가슴에 달아드리면
옅은 미소로 조용히 껴안아 주던
나의 어머니

아무리 카네이션을 무덤 앞에 갖다 놓아도
한없이 슬퍼지는 내 마음
어머니 얼굴만 안개처럼 피어오를 뿐
앞이 잘 보이지 않는다

On a day full of freshness
The season I want to love passes by in silence
Alone in front of the grave
"Mother! I love you!"
In a voice mixed with crying
I shout out while being choked

싱그러움이 가득한 날
사랑하고 싶은 계절은 말없이 흘러가고
나 홀로 무덤 앞에
"어머니! 사랑합니다"
울음 섞인 음성으로
목메어 외쳐본다

The Day I Miss You

I anxiously miss you, but
Rather, I come to hate you.

Even if I look into the fog
You are invisible
Smiling, the sky
Covers my eyes with clouds

I still hate you today, too
I should not recall you any more
Somehow, as time goes by
Your face becomes clearer
I come to hate the longing I feel

When I look into the old spring
Your smiling face is seen
Is it because I still can't forget you?

너 보고 싶은 날

보고파 애타는 마음인데
오히려 보기 싫어진다

안개 속을 쳐다봐도
보이지 않는 너
하늘이 씩 웃으며
구름으로 나의 눈을 가린다

오늘도 보기 싫은 너
다시는 생각이 나지 않아야 할 텐데
어쩐지 시간이 흐를수록
더욱 또렷해지는 얼굴
그리움조차 싫어진다

오래된 옹달샘을 들여다보면
너의 미소 띤 얼굴이 보이는 이유는
아직도 너를 잊지 못함 인가

Although I don't know where you are now
Even your voice
Even a little bit through the phone
I don't want to hear

지금 어디에 있는지 모르지만
너의 음성이라도
폰을 통해서 조금이라도
듣고 싶지 않다

Rain That Wets My Heart

My longing for you pouring down as rain
Seeps into my heart

Worried that my longing will get wet in the rain
I open the umbrella in my heart

Darkening sky
The blue sky seen between the clouds
Is your heart

After erasing the day with rain
I draw
My longing for you in that place

If I put rainwater in my heart, in the moisture of its chambers,
I sow flower seeds
I imagine your flowers blooming

가슴을 적시는 비

비가 되어 쏟아지는 그대 그리움이
내 마음에 스며든다

그리움이 비에 젖을까 걱정되어
마음속 우산을 펴본다

어두워지는 하늘
구름 사이 파랗게 보이는 하늘은
당신의 마음

빗물로 하루를 지우고
그 자리에 그대 그리움을
그려 본다

마음에 빗물 담아 촉촉한 가슴에
꽃씨 뿌리면
당신의 꽃이 활짝 피어나는 것을 상상해 본다

Cheoseo

Do you hear?
In the night when crickets cry
The sound of my breathing approaches over the fallen leaves

In the deep sky sprinkled with jade paint
Falling clouds and a cappuccino sunset
Do you see them?

In the wind that passes by my earlobes
The whispering and excited hearts of lovers
Do you feel them?

Cheoseo, the mosquito that was waking you
from a sweet sleep with an exciting buzz, on a tropical night
Should leave as their mouths are crooked.
Do you know it?

처서

들리나요?
귀뚜라미 우는 밤
낙엽 넘어 다가가는 나의 숨소리

비취 물감 뿌려놓은 깊은 하늘에
풍덩 빠지는 뭉게구름 카푸치노 노을이
보이나요?

귓불 스치는 바람결에
소곤대며 들뜬 연인의 가슴을
느끼나요?

열대야에 신나게 윙윙대며 단잠 깨우던
모기가 입이 삐뚤어져 떠나야 하는 처서를
아는가요?

In the approaching typhoon
I have the wisdom to pack my nest
With the eyes of an eagle looking high above
Before playing with the colorful autumn leaves

울긋불긋 단풍놀이하기 전
다가오는 태풍에
높이 떠 살피는 매의 눈으로
둥지 싸매는 지혜를 가져본다

Autumn Sky

The sky so blue that it is cold
Is blue to be cold?

The sky where even the clouds turned blue
If I throw a pebble
Like ripples in a quiet pond
Will it be finely cracked round?
Like frost on a car window
Will it flow down in pieces?
With a nervous heart
I look at the blue sky pathetically

가을 하늘

시리도록 푸른 하늘
차갑도록 푸르다

구름도 파랗게 변해 버린 하늘
조약돌 하나 던지면
고요한 연못의 파문처럼
둥글게 둥글게 실금이 갈까
차창에 서린 서릿발처럼
조각으로 흘러내릴까
조마조마한 마음으로
푸른 하늘을 애처롭게 쳐다본다

Leaf Letters

At the scent of roses that flows clearly
When I close my eyes, you are visible

When I look up at the sky
Because I want to see your fresh smile
Tears linger in the empty area
Of the longing that has been pieced together

Trees hug warmly and offer comfort
The pain like a dagger
Rests in my bosom
As red flowers

I put it all in the blue wind
And attach a stamp where white wild roses are drawn
To send my ardent heart
To you

나뭇잎 편지

맑게 흐르는 장미 향기에
눈을 감으면 당신이 보입니다

싱그러운 미소가 보고 싶어
하늘을 우러러보면
조각조각 이어놓은 그리움
텅 빈 곳에 눈물이 맴돕니다

눈물이 비수 같은 아픔을
따뜻하게 안아서 다독이고
빨간 꽃으로
내 가슴에 안깁니다

푸른 바람 담아
하얀 찔레꽃 그려진 우표를 붙여
애틋한 내 마음을
당신께 보내드립니다

Coffee

A day when autumn rain unfortunately falls
Autumn drinks a cup of coffee
The coffee cup left alone feels lonely

The oak tree standing on the roadside
Wrapped in the autumn wind
No matter how much it shouts
It could not avoid the rainwater
So that the window is dripping wet
At the side of the window, only the coffee that has been cooled
Shivers due to loneliness

커피

가을비 아쉽게 내리는 날
가을이 커피를 마신다
혼자 남겨진 커피잔은 고독을 느낀다

도롯가에 서 있는 떡갈나무
가을바람에 휘감긴 채
아무리 고함쳐도
다가온 빗물을 피하지 못해
흠뻑 젖은 유리창 가에서
식어버린 커피만
외로움에 떤다

Chapter 5
Scene of a Ball

제5장
무도회의 풍경

Scene of a Ball

As life came riding the light
The girl opened the door of crying to come out
Into a new world where even judgment is difficult

Soft skin and intelligent eyes
On the beautifully decorated stage
The entire surroundings are decorated with gems such as sapphires.

When she stands on tiptoes and spins around with white skirt,
The song of the ball is felt; exciting by the young heart.

In a world that spins
With unstoppable dances
Bees and butterflies covered with faded blood come
The innocent girl needed a mask

무도회의 풍경

생명이 빛을 타고 들어와
판단조차 어려운 새로운 세상에
울음의 문을 열고 나온 소녀

부드러운 피부에 총명한 눈빛
예쁘게 단장된 무대에는
온통 주위가 사파이어 같은 보석으로 꾸며져 있다

발끝을 세우고 하얀 치마폭으로 한 바퀴 휙 돌면
어린 가슴에는 무도회의 노래가 흥겨워진다

멈출 수 없는 춤으로
돌아가는 세상에
퇴색된 피를 묻혀 오는 벌·나비들
순진한 소녀는 가면이 필요했다

After embroidering the clean bed sheet with beautiful passion
Eyes meeting each other dance a dance of joy
Towards an endlessly high place.

The unstoppable waltz of the ball
In it, faces are hidden
Refinement is expressed as pretense
The sadness due to the empty dignity that is being raised.
Becomes the shame that sticks thickly
On the body that hasn't been washed for weeks

The ball still continues
Worn-out clothes and wrinkles on the crushed face
Cannot be hidden no matter how hard she tries to hide
Her sighs become a song and spread gradually

Waltz danced while holding hands at the ball
A leg standing on one toe maintains balance
And the other leg is extended fully outward and rotates,
To ride on a beautiful melody on stage.

깨끗한 침대보에 아름다운 정열로 수놓고
맞닿는 눈길은 끝없이 높은 곳을 향하여
환희의 춤을 추기도 한다

멈출 수 없는 무도회의 왈츠
그 속에는 얼굴을 가리고
교양을 가식으로 표출하며
높여가는 공허한 품위에 서글픔은
수 주일 동안 씻지 못한 몸에
덕지덕지 붙어있는 수치심이 된다

아직도 계속되는 무도회
낡아버린 복장과 쭈그러진 얼굴의 주름
가리고 가려도 어쩔 수 없이
한숨이 노래 되어 점점 퍼지고 있다

무도회에 서로 손을 잡고 추는 왈츠
한쪽 발끝을 세운 다리가 균형을 잡고
다른 다리는 밖으로 힘껏 뻗어 회전을 하면
무대 위에서 아름다운 선율을 타게 된다

On the stage of life where the ball comes to an end
There is nothing but regret and remorse
Oh, the conversations and the dances
Although all were thought to rise to art, but
She is falling into a hot swamp from which she can never
rise again

무도회가 스르르 막을 내리는 생生의 무대에는
덩그러니 후회와 회한뿐
오, 대화와 춤들
모든 것이 예술로 상승할 줄 알았으나
다시는 올라오지 못할 뜨거운 늪에 빠지고 있다

White Heart

From early morning.
White snow has been falling

Pure white snow falling on my shoulders all night long
Covers even the painful fault, and
Covers my heart with white clothes

Since at least in a snowy night
I would like to live white
I pick up a brush and draw a white heart

하얀 마음

이른 아침부터 .
하얀 눈이 흩날리고 있다

밤새도록 어깨 위에 내리는 새하얀 눈
괴로운 허물마저 덮고
내 마음을 흰옷으로 덮는다

눈이 펑펑 내리는 밤이라도
나는 하얗게 살고 싶어
붓을 들고 하얀 마음을 그려 본다

Train Trip

Carrying the past
While dreaming of joy and happiness amid expectations and wishes
A train running toward the future

Giving myself to the sound of the wheels vibrating
Even trying to sleep although it is hard
I am endeavoring to be lost in deep contemplation.

At least for the limited time in life
In a rusty train running over time
Sometimes looking at the scenery outside
I retrace memories

Sprinkled on the railroad tracks
Heartbreaking regrets
Although life is a one-way run, but
It passes by as fast as the speeding train

기차여행

과거를 싣고
기대와 바램 속에 기쁨과 행복을 꿈꾸며
미래를 향해 달리는 기차

바퀴의 진동 소리에 몸을 맡기고
오지 않는 잠까지 청하며
깊은 사색에 잠기려 애쓰고 있다

인생의 한정된 시간이라도
세월 위를 달리는 녹슨 열차 속에서
가끔 바깥 경치를 구경하며
추억을 더듬는다

철로 위에 뿌려진
가슴앓이하는 회한들
편도만 달리는 인생이지만
기차의 속력만큼 빠르게 지나친다

With a ticket to the final station

A journey that runs on a track that does not get off at a simple station.

The train only sounds a whistle, whether it knows my heart or not.

종착역까지 가는 승차권을 가지고
혹여나 간이역에 내리지 않게 달리는 여행
기차는 내 마음을 아는지 모르는지 기적만 울린다

Yellow Bean Leaves

I neatly trimmed the leaves one by one, and
Pickled in salt water

The pretty bodies dyed in yellow
Are added with delicious seasoning

Engraved on yellow bean leaves
Thoughts of you
Only memories are accumulated neatly

With a spoonful of boiled rice that will be enjoyed
I take out old memories one by one
To add to the taste of the food made by mom
To my kids too.

노란 콩잎

한 잎 두 잎 차곡차곡 손질해
소금물에 절였다

노란 색깔에 물든 예쁜 몸매
맛깔스러운 양념을 덧칠한다

노란 콩잎에 새겨진
그대 생각
추억들만 차곡차곡 쌓여 간다

맛있게 먹을 쌀밥 한 숟가락으로
옛 기억 하나둘 꺼내어
엄마가 해 주던 그 맛을
내 아이들에게도 얹어준다

Lombardia Wine

It rains all day
Drinking while leaning against the window
A glass of sparkling wine is good.

Rain streaks stroking the glass window
Remind me of the touch of him I met in the past.
So much so, that I now tightly hold the glass I am holding.

When I gather a sip slowly in my mouth,
Warmth spreads throughout my body
In a sea of rich tannin
A light humming comes out naturally.

When swallowing it into the throat
A confession of first love
Of which the first word that was hardly said, is formed on my lips.

롬바르디아Lombardia 포도주

종일 비가 내린다
창가에 기대어 마시는
스파클링 와인 한잔이 좋다.

유리창을 쓰다듬는 빗줄기가
지난날 만났던 그 사람 손길이 생각나
들고 있는 잔을 꼭 쥐게 된다

한 모금을 천천히 입안에 모으면
따스함이 온몸에 퍼지고
풍부한 탄닌 바디감에
저절로 나오는 가벼운 허밍

목 안으로 삼킬 때
첫마디를 꺼내기가 어려웠던
첫사랑의 고백을 내뱉게 된다.

In front of my gently closed eyes
A faint face
Comes together with the sound of rain

Is it the scent of the one I want to see?
Or a whisper of days gone by?
A fresh scent penetrates my heart

On a day like today
Lombardia, full of elegant flavors
Sparkling wine is good.

살포시 감은 눈앞에는
희미한 얼굴이
빗소리와 함께 찾아 든다

보고픈 이의 향기일까?
지나간 날의 속삭임일까?
상큼한 향이 내 가슴에 파고든다

오늘 같은 날에는
우아한 풍미가 깃든 롬바르디아Lombardia
스파클링 와인이 좋다

Insensitivity

For consecutive works, thoughtlessly, the squirrel
Spins the treadmill habitually
It's not a given obligation
The only reason is being alive

Today, not different from yesterday
About tomorrow that will come
I
became insensitive without excitement

Not knowing that I missed the difficult steps
The stupidity
Makes me lag behind, to my regret

Daily life to pour the tea
And drink the tea holding the teacup
The scent of tea permeating into the whole body
Has become a formality, like a habit.

무감각

연속된 일에 다람쥐는 생각 없이
습관적으로 쳇바퀴를 돌리는
주어진 의무도 아니고
살아있다는 이유뿐이다

오늘도 어제와 다르지 않게
다가올 내일을
설렘 없이 무감각해진
나

힘겨운 발걸음을 헛디딘 줄 모르는
아둔함이
나를 뒤처지게 해서 아쉽기만 하다

차를 따라
찻잔을 쥐고 차를 마시는 일상
온몸에 스며드는 차향
습관처럼 형식이 되어버렸다

Last Night in the Bed of Boomin

The day coming to an end
Kisses the sunset

Bitter tasting
A cup of coffee
It's a solemn day to look back
The years that embraced my whole body

Even if I fill it and empty it again
The same daily life continues endlessly
At least yesterday and today
I want to be remembered with different memories

Leaving the bed at Bumin Hospital
At the thought about my home to which I will return tomorrow
Even if I try to sleep soundly
Only my heart is beating.

부민 침상의 마지막 밤

저물어가는 하루
노을에 입을 맞춘다

쓴맛이 나는
커피 한잔
온몸을 감싸 안았던 세월을
뒤돌아보는 숙연한 날이다

다시 채우고 비워 봐도
끝없이 계속되는 똑같은 일상
지난날과 오늘만은
다른 추억으로 기억되고 싶다

부민병원의 침상을 떠나
내일이면 돌아갈 집 생각에
푸근히 잠을 청해도
내 마음만 두근대고 있다

White Snow

Snow that came in pure white
Hug me tightly

What is the joy that has come?
It creates a white world
The snow that falls because it misses me

Is heaped up gradually
In my heart.

I would like to put the feeling of stepping on it in my ear
And the cold feeling in my heart
And make it melt with love

Snow that will disappear tomorrow
Today
The snow that brought joy has felt good

Although the snow that came white
Leaves cold
The heart that stays in my hometown is just happy

하얀 눈

순백으로 찾아온 눈
나를 꼬옥 껴안는다

찾아온 기쁨이 무엇인지
하얀 세상을 만들어
내가 보고파 내리는 눈

내 가슴에
소복소복 쌓이고 있다

밟은 느낌은 귀에 담고
시린 느낌은 마음에 담아
사랑으로 녹아내리게 하고 싶다

내일 되면 없어질 눈
오늘
즐거움을 데리고 온 눈이 착하게 느낀다

하얗게 찾아온 눈이
아무리 차가움을 남긴다 해도
고향에 머무른 마음은 행복할 뿐이다

Pine Knots

Containing regrettable stories
The voice got hoarse while telling
Due to the hardship of life with woe and tumult
Cracked tortoiseshell

After the clear wind passes by
Between the leaves lying on their sides
The servant bird, ssokdok, ssokdok, chattering
Passes by

The wound, which is hurting even when crying
Even if I want to sew it
The wind only strokes the pine knots

소나무 옹이

한 많은 사연 담고
토해내다 목은 쉬고
풍진의 세파에
갈라 터진 거북 등

맑은 바람 스친 뒤
모로 돌아누운 잎새 사이
머슴 새 쏙독 쏙독 지껄이며
지나간다

울어도 아픈 상처
꿰매 주고 싶어도
바람은 소나무 옹이만 어루만진다

Sunday

On Friday afternoon, my heart flutters
I love Sunday
When I can be lazy and relax

In exchange for salary
Days filled with labor
Emotions and feelings are wasted

Although it is compensation for what was wasted
In an attempt to endure economic times
It's a good time to recharge

It's the only gift that can recharge
Back-bending toil and dry labor
A tightly packed week

일요일

금요일 오후면 가슴이 설레다가
게으름 피우고 여유 부릴 수
있는 일요일을 사랑한다

봉급과 맞바꾸어
노동으로 채워진 날들
감성과 감정은 탕진된다

경제적 시간을 견뎌내려
탕진된 것에 대한 보상이지만
재충전하기 좋은 시간이다

등이 휘는 수고와 메마른 노동
빽빽이 짜인 한 주간을
재충전할 수 있는 유일한 선물이다

Say Hello Due to Longing

In the deep sea
Floating around all day
A cloud-like longing

The person I miss and want to say, "hello" to
In some sky
He should bloom as a cloud flower

Scratched by harsh rain and wind
The old days
Since traces of countless fallen fruits
Remain in my memory as a vivid pain
I cannot but shake my head.

As if nothing happened
In the pile of broken stones next to the dented wall,
When covered with moss, and
Even the fallen grass stands up again
Rose moss flowers are blooming in droves.

그리움에 안부를 묻다

깊은 바다에
온종일 둥둥 떠다니는
구름 같은 그리움

안부를 묻고 싶은 그리운 사람
어느 하늘엔가
구름 꽃으로 피어나겠지

모진 비바람이 할퀴고 간
지난날
무수히 떨궈진 낙과의 흔적들이
선명한 통증으로 기억 속에 남아있어
고개를 절레절레 흔들 수밖에 없다

아무 일 없다는 듯
패인 담장 옆 허물어진 돌무더기에는
이끼가 덮이고
넘어진 풀들도 다시 일어서면
채송화꽃이 다투어 피고 있다

Trials buried by time
Sometimes remain like stepping stones, but
The heart that remembers the pain
Revives like neuralgia

Disappearing to somewhere beyond the foot of a distant mountain
Hidden in a bunch of clouds
I,
Go in search of white longing

세월에 묻힌 시련
디딤돌 같이 남기도 하지만
통증이 기억나는 마음은
신경통처럼 되살아난다

먼 산자락 너머 어디론가 사라지는
한 무더기 구름 속으로 숨어버린
나,
하얀 그리움을 찾아 나선다

Colored Leaves

A beautifully colored leaf that fell
I pick up

How did it live
Was it colored so beautifully?

When I look at it for quite a while
My life is seen.

In what color
Is it getting colored?
I'm increasingly curious

물든 나뭇잎

곱게 물들어 떨어진 나뭇잎 하나
주워 든다

어떻게 살았기에
이렇게 아름답게 물들었을까

한참 동안 들여다보면
내 삶이 보인다

어떤 색으로
물들고 있을까
갈수록 궁금하다

Living in Loneliness

Greeting each day
Emotions change easily, but
At least my heart
Accompanies my loneliness

Not just said with the mouth
Due to the loneliness that is often embraced in my heart
Like walking alone at night
There are times when I feel solitary and lonely.

Even when the empty field wiped by cold becomes desolate
Wrapping loneliness with my two arms
I am walking down the road with a warm heart.

외로움에 살아가며

하루하루를 맞아
감정이 쉽게 변해도
내 마음만은
외로움과 동행을 한다

입으로만 말하는 것이 아닌
가슴에 품을 때가 많은 외로움에
홀로 밤길을 걷는 것처럼
쓸쓸하고 고독해질 때가 있다

추위가 훑고 간 빈들이 황량하게 되어도
나는 외로움을 두 팔로 감싸며
따뜻한 마음으로 길을 걸어가고 있다

Epilogue

A song of life projected at the ball

발문

무도회에서 투영된 삶의 노래

<Epilogue>

A song of life projected at the ball

- After reading the collection of poems of poet, Young Hee Han's 『Scene of Ball』 -

Won Chul Choi (Professor Emeritus, Pusan National University, poet, essayist)

Poet Young Hee Han is a poet rich in leisurely sensibility. The poet was born as the youngest of two sons and four daughters in the beautiful garden-like countryside of Ulju-gun, Ulsan city.

She lives while singing about her life, projected in a quiet environment. In her eyes, the rural scenery was the melody of a beautiful song, and the footprints of her long journey were like musical notes playing on music paper. She is a poet who transformed the phenomena occurring there, into poetry.

Poet Young Hee Han says, "After putting aside shallow ideas in front of nature/ I listen to the language of the universe in silence" So, the poet sings, "When dawn comes in the countryside,

<발문>

무도회에서 투영된 삶의 노래

- 한영희 시인의 시집 『무도회의 풍경』을 읽고 -

최원철 (부산대학교 명예교수, 시인, 수필가)

한영희 시인은 여유로운 감성이 풍부한 시인이다. 시인은 울산시 울주군의 아름다운 정원과 같은 시골에서 2남 4녀 중 막내로 태어났다.

시인은 고요한 환경에서 투영되어 오는 삶을 노래하며 산다. 그의 눈에는 시골의 풍경이 아름다운 노래의 멜로디였고 살아온 긴 여정의 발자국들이 오선지 위를 뛰어노는 음표와 같이 거기에서 일어나는 현상을 시詩로 바꾸어 놓은 시인이다.

한영희 시인은 "자연 앞에서 얄팍한 생각일랑 접고/침묵 속에서 우주의 언어를 듣는다". 그래서 시인은 "시골의 새벽이 되면 시詩도 잠에서 깨어나기 시작한다" (새벽을 여는 시골 中)고 노래한다. 그뿐 아니다. "텃밭에 내리는 비"가 "일손을 바쁘게"하지만 "비를 피해/처마 끝에 숨어들면/여유로운 시골의 풍경이 그려진다" (농사꾼의 하루 中)라고 했다. 여기에서 시골의 여유로운 풍경을 그리는 시인의 마음을 볼 수 있다.

even poetry begins to wake up from sleep" (from Countryside at the break of dawn). In addition, she said, "The rain falling on the vegetable garden,", "To make the working hands busy," but "to avoid the rain/When I hide at the edge of eaves/ A leisurely rural scene comes to mind" (from A Day of Farmers). Here, you can see the poet's mind depicting the leisurely scene of the countryside.

Poet Han Young-hee writes most of the poems in Chapter 1, 『Countryside at the break of dawn』, as poems that are ordinary but can be easily and quickly understood.

The countryside where the poet lived is where everyone enjoys nature, and the countryside full of warmheartedness is expressed in her poetry.

Having fresh greens
In the countryside fifth-day market
Sellers are generous

The smell of a country market that has been familiar since ancient times
Of the savory anchovy stock
Crisscrosses the alleys of the fifth-day market

한영희 시인은 제1장 『새벽을 여는 시골』에 대한 대부분의 시詩가 평범하면서도 쉽고 빠르게 이해를 할 수 있는 시詩를 쓰고 있다.

시인이 살았던 시골은 누구나가 평범하게 자연을 즐기며, 인정이 듬뿍 들어있는 시골을 자신의 시詩에서 묻어나고 있다.

싱싱한 푸성귀가 있는
시골 오일장
인심이 두둑하다

예부터 익숙한 시골 장터 냄새는
구수한 멸칫국물로
오일장의 골목 안을 누빈다

Placed on fine noodles
Stir-fried in sesame oil
Pumpkin garnish
Slurp, the noodles are eaten like a storm in an instant

When I emptied a bowl of noodles
The ample satiety for 5,000 won
Makes me happy

Before I know
There is a long line of people in front of the tasty restaurant.

When I was late only 5 minutes, I would miss the happy taste
Sometimes I was startled.

Exchanged at the countryside market
The warm heart
Makes even the cold weather warm

- Full text of 「Banquet Noodles at a Rural Market」

In the poem above, the scene of fifth-day markets, which have been passed down as a unique rural culture in Korea, is well depicted. It makes it easy to feel sympathy for the banquet noodles

고운 면발에 얹어 놓은
참기름에 볶아 낸
낭개의 고명
후루룩 삽시간에 폭풍 흡입이 일어난다

국수 한 그릇 비우면
오천 원에 두둑한 포만감은
나를 기쁘게 한다

어느덧
맛집 앞에는 사람들의 줄이 길다

5분만 늦었으면 행복한 맛을
놓칠까 아찔할 때도 있었다

시골 장에서 주고받는
따뜻한 마음은
차가운 날씨조차 훈훈하게 한다

- 「시골장의 잔치국수」의 전문

위의 시詩에서 한국의 특유한 시골 문화처럼 전해 내려오는 오일장의 풍경을 잘 나타내고 있다. 시골 장터에서 볼 수 있는 잔치국수에 대한 연민의 정을 쉽게 느끼게 한다. 여기에서 "따뜻한

that can be found in rural markets. Here, the countryside is where "warm hearts" make "even the cold weather warm."

Furthermore, poet Young Hee Han recalls the first full moon of the first lunar month in her hometown. She unfolds the scene of various families eating five-grain rice and intending to start everything of a year. The poet reflects on her memories of the first full moon of the year as follows.

Under the moonlight startled by the sound of biting on a nut to ward off boils
A glass of ear-quickening wine to give away the heat
The memories of drinking it happily are fresh.

Five-grain rice with seasoned wild vegetables
Stew with frozen pollack and tofu
Sunshine and wind falling on the top of the mountain
Children running around dropping leaves
The day of the first full moon of the lunar year is gradually getting busier.

When the season that brought the warm breeze
Hung spring on a tree
A warm affection seeps into my heart.

마음”들이 “차가운 날씨조차 훈훈하게” 만드는 것이 시골이다.

더 나아가 한영희 시인은 고향의 정월대보름을 회상한다. 여러 가정에서 오곡밥을 먹으며 한해의 모든 일을 시작하려는 광경을 펼쳐 보인다. 시인은 정월 대보름의 추억을 아래와 같이 되새긴다.

부름 깨무는 소리에 놀란 달빛 아래
더위를 팔던 귀밝이술 한잔
기쁘게 마시던 추억이 새롭다

오곡밥에 산채나물
동태에 두부 넣은 찌게
산꼭대기에 내리는 햇살과 바람
잎새를 떨구며 나대던 아이들
대보름은 점점 바빠진다

훈풍을 몰고 온 계절이
나무에 봄을 매달면
내 마음에는 따스한 정이 스민다

Built a bonfire
Performed a ritual to Earth God viewing the moon
Beating a gong
Signaled the day of the first full moon of the lunar year
The old days are missed today
- Full text of 「The Day of the First Full Moon of the Lunar Year」

Rather than expressing the journey that takes place at the ball of her life as lament or sadness, poet Young Hee Han gives us a glimpse into her heart as she walks toward a hopeful tomorrow. "Until the end of life/ When a dark night will come/So that neither moonlight/ Nor starlight will be visible/ I will walk even a dark road" (from Walk Following the Starlight). Also, on the day of the first full moon of the lunar year, "Built a bonfire/Performed a ritual to Earth God viewing the moon/Beating a gong/Signaled the day of the first full moon of the lunar year/The old days are missed today" (from "The Full Moon of the New Year"). This is a longing and memory that cannot be felt by city dwellers.

Poet Young Hee Han says, "I count the time/That dragged/My life thus far." "... Forgotten while being flitted by winds/Memories/...
Sometimes in regret/Sometimes in joy" (from Between Seasons)

모닥불 피워놓고
달맞이에 지신 밟고
꽹과리 두드리며
정월대보름을 알리던
옛날이 그리운 오늘이다

- 「정월대보름」의 전문

한영희 시인은 삶의 무도회에서 일어나는 여정을 한탄이나 비애로 표현하기보다 희망찬 내일을 향하여 걸어가는 마음을 엿볼 수 있다. "달빛도/별빛도 보이지 않는/어두운 밤이 찾아오는/생의 마지막까지/캄캄한 길이라도 걸어야겠다" (별빛 따라 걷는다 中). 또한, 정월 대보름날에 "모닥불 피워놓고/달맞이에 지신 밟고/꽹과리 두드리며/정월대보름을 알리던/옛날이 그리운 오늘이다" (정월대보름 中) 이것은 도회지 사람으로서는 느낄 수 없는 그리움이며 추억이다.

한영희 시인은 "지금까지 끌고 온/세월을 헤아려본다". "...바람에 스치며 잊고 있었던/추억들/....... 때로는 후회에/때로는 기쁨에" (계절과 계절 사이 中) 아무 잡념 없이 여로를 한 걸음 한 걸음

indicating that as she walks step by step on her journey without any distracting thoughts, her heart becomes audacious. This is the memory of happiness that one feels every time the seasons change in rural life.

I would like to further recommend that her poetry metaphorically expresses the intuitive perception of the object. Rather than directly expressing what one sees and feels, poetry should strive to reveal the beauty or secrets hidden behind it, or the meaning that others have not been able to find.

While poet Young Hee Han sang about the warmheartedness and customs of the countryside in which she has lived thus far, in Chapter 2, "Comma of Summer," she looks back on her life in her shape taking a break in the ball of life and tells the journey of life like a personal ball after placing it on the stage.

A hot and hard asphalt road and
A leisurely country road
Are in contrast with each other

In the countryside, the sound of unknown grass bugs.
Open the road leisurely, and
Even birds walk as companions

걸으며 마음이 두둑해진다고 토로하고 있다. 이것이 시골 생활에 있어서 계절과 계절이 바뀔 때마다 느끼는 행복의 추억인 것이다.

시詩에는 대상에 대한 직관적 인식을 은유적으로 나타내는 것을 더욱 추천하고 싶다. 시詩는 보고 느끼는 것을 곧이곧대로 표현하는 것 보다 그 뒤에 숨겨진 아름다움이나 비밀 또는 다른 이들이 찾아내지 못한 의미를 드러내는 데 노력해야 할 것이다.

한영희 시인이 지금까지 살아온 시골의 인정이나 관습을 노래했는가 하면 제2장 『여름의 쉼표』 에서는 삶의 무도회에서 잠시 쉬어가는 모습에서 자신의 삶을 뒤돌아보기도 하고 개인의 무도회와 같은 삶의 여정을 무대 위에 놓고 이야기를 한다.

뜨겁고 딱딱한 아스팔트 길과
유유자적한 시골길이
대조가 된다

시골에는 알 수 없는 풀벌레 소리
한가롭게 길을 열고
새들도 길동무 삼아 걸음을 옮긴다

The footsteps with a crunch speak of the texture of the soil.
At the scent of roses blooming in hot summer
I draw a comma for a while

Under the cool shade provided by the trees
Hidden pleasure
Steps on a country road are leisurely.

- Full text of 「Comma of Summer」

In the poem above, the poet indicates that there is a difference of leisure in the contrast between the numerous cars passing by busily, raising a lot of dust on the asphalt road and the hot and melting asphalt road in the city in the summer, and the leisurely appearance of the country road. In addition, the poet sings that the leisurely scenery of hearing the sounds of insects and birds singing, stepping on the dirt, and smelling the scent of roses is a hidden pleasure.

She comically expresses the thoughts that everyone feels about their beloved husband in the poet's leisurely life. The poet's husband runs a company and is said to love his wife very much

사박사박 발걸음은 흙의 질감을 말하고
뜨거운 여름에 피어나는 장미 향기에
잠깐 쉼표를 그려 본다

나무가 내어 주는 시원한 그늘에
숨겨진 즐거움
시골길 걸음이 여유롭다

- 「여름의 쉼표」 의 전문

위의 시詩에서 시인은 도회지의 아스팔트 길에는 여름이 되면 많은 먼지를 일으키며 바쁘게 지나다니는 수많은 자동차, 또한 뜨겁고 녹아내리는 아스팔트 길과 시골길의 유유자적한 모습들이 대조되는 여유의 차이가 있다. 그뿐만 아니라 풀벌레 소리와 새들의 노랫소리를 듣고 흙을 밟으며 장미 향기를 맡는 여유로운 풍경이 숨겨진 즐거움이라고 시인은 노래하고 있다.

시인의 여유로운 삶에서 사랑하는 남편에 대해 누구나 느끼고 있는 생각을 코믹할 정도로 표출하고 있다. 시인의 남편은 회사를 경영하고 있는 분이며 몹시 바쁜 생활 가운데 아내를 너무나

despite his extremely busy life. In the poem titled, "Husband," she refers to the husband as a person with whom she has a "strange degree of kinship, which is neither father nor brother." These days, it is common to see young women in South Korea sometimes calling their future husbands, 'brother.' Here we can read the language of an era that is rapidly changing. At first it changed from, 'honey, you' to 'darling' and eventually to, 'brother'. Seeing this, it is difficult for older people to accept it, and our world has become a world where people who point out such words are called, 'oldies'. Therefore, the poet defines her husband as, "a person who is both close and distant." So, if you try to explain further after reading the full text of the poet's "Husband," it would be making an unnecessary addition.

A strange degree of kinship, which is neither father nor brother
A person who is both close and distant
With whom I discuss closely sometimes
And I cannot talk other times

Sometimes hurts me to the extent to be thought to be an enemy.
But sometimes can easily say that he loves me the most
The man

사랑하고 있다고 한다. 시詩의 제목 「남편」 에서, 남편을 "아빠도 아니고 오빠도 아닌 이상한 촌수"의 관계를 맺은 사람이라고 말한다. 요즘 우리나라에서 젊은 여인들이 남편 될 사람을 가끔 '오빠'라고 부르는 것을 흔히 볼 수 있다. 여기에서 우리는 빠르게 변천 되어 오는 시대의 언어를 읽을 수 있다. 처음엔 '여보, 당신'에서 '자기'로 변하더니 급기야 '오빠'로 변했다. 이것을 보면 늙은이들은 수용하기가 어렵고 이런 말을 지적하면 '꼰대'라고 일컫는 세상이 되었다. 그래서 "가깝고도 먼 사람"으로 스스로 규정을 짓는다. 그래서 시인의 「남편」 이라는 시편의 전문을 읽고 더 이상 설명하려 들면 오히려 사족을 붙이는 셈이 된다.

아빠도 아니고 오빠도 아닌 이상한 촌수
어떨 땐 가깝게 의논하다가
말할 수 없는
가깝고도 먼 사람

원수인가 싶도록 마음 상하다가
가장 사랑한다고 쉽게 말할 수 있는
남자

As time goes by
The person who even taught me war

A wildly strange person
Who is hateful sometimes but becomes favorite other times
A strange person
With whom I cook dinner and eat together today too.

- Full text of "Husband"

Husband is an antinomic partner in my life, someone who can be said to be a very hateful person sometimes and can be said to be a person loved at other times. This is not the only thing. As time goes by and the relationship becomes irrelevant, the husband is the one with whom one even wages war rather than any courtesy or comfort. Husband is, "A wildly strange person/Who is hateful sometimes but becomes favorite other times". Isn't he sometimes felt like a "strange person"?

Poet Young Hee Han is maturing into a complete life through the process of reconciling pain and love in various ways, accepting everything despite the waves of confused thoughts, and realizing life one by one.

시간이 흐를수록
나에게 전쟁까지 가르쳐 주는 사람

싫다가도 좋아지는
걷잡을 수 없이 묘한 사람
오늘도 저녁을 지어서 함께 먹는
이상한 사람

- 「남편」의 전문

남편이 어떨 때는 매우 미운 사람이다가 또 어떨 때는 사랑한다고 말할 수 있는 삶의 이율배반적인 상대이다. 이것만이 아니다. 시간이 흘러 관계가 무관해질 때는 어떤 예의나 위로보다 전쟁까지 하게 되는 사람이 남편인 것이다. "싫다가도 좋아지는/
걷잡을 수 없이 묘한 사람"이며, 가끔 "이상한 사람"이라고 느끼고 있지 않는가?

한영희 시인은 아픔과 사랑을 다양하게 화해해 가며 혼란한 생각의 물결 속에서도 모든 것을 수용하면서 인생의 삶을 하나씩 깨달으며 사는 과정이 완전한 인생의 삶으로 성숙해 가고 있다.

Poet Young Hee Han's poems always embrace the leisurely nature of the pure life in the countryside in her heart. Even when she takes a break when the dance has reached its peak as she has been rushing through life in a hectic manner, she is reflecting on how leisurely her life has been. Looking at, "Leisurely Early Summer," among her poems,

Spring was nice because it was spring, but
These days added with heat
Are filled with a fine scent

Although always busy and things that must be done are overflowing
When the roses over the fence smile
The scent of acacia flowers is delicate

Lettuce and crown daisy that grow well verdantly
All kinds of abundance
Come into my eyes

In a state of nature
The sun-drenched streets are getting hotter
There are cold winters too

한영희 시인의 시편들은 시골의 순수한 삶이 있는 여유로운 자연을 항상 가슴에 안고 산다. 정신없이 삶의 길을 달려와서 어느 정도 무도회가 절정에 다다랐을 때 잠시 쉬어가는 순간에도 자신의 삶이 얼마나 여유롭게 살았는지를 성찰하고 있다. 그의 시편 가운데 「여유로운 초여름」을 살펴보면

봄은 봄이라서 좋았지만
더위까지 겹친 요즘
고운 향기로 채워진다

늘 바빠할 일이 넘쳐나지만
담장 너머엔 장미가 웃으면
아카시아 꽃향기가 은은하다

파릇파릇 잘 자라는 상추와 쑥갓
온갖 풍성함이
눈에 들어온다

자연 그대로
햇살 내려앉은 거리가 더워지고
차가운 겨울도 있다

What beautiful seasons
Even for my mind and body that get tired easily,
I look for a place to rest leisurely

- Full text of 「Leisurely Early Summer」

The poet might have written this poem comparing herself to when she was at the peak of her maturity, to early summer. When she looks back on her past after spending her maidenhood without knowing much, she realizes that there are more beautiful things that happened to her than things that she has done wrong to others. Therefore, she makes you feel that days carried a beautiful scent until the early summer, when the heat comes. The poet's life was full of hectic activities, but when her neighbors ("roses over the fence") envied her, the poet sang that her life was as gentle as the sweet "scent of acacia flowers."

And the poet foretells her future. After early summer, she guesses that the abundance of lettuce and crown daisy will come in the fall, and then she thinks about the coming cold winter. All of these have been sublimated into "beautiful seasons" and now she is "looking for a resting place to rest leisurely/Even for my mind and body that get tired easily."

참으로 아름다운 계절들
쉬이 지치는 정신과 몸에도
여유롭게 쉬어 갈 쉼터를 찾는다

- 「여유로운 초여름」의 전문

시인이 한창 성숙한 시기의 자신을 초여름에 빗대어 시詩를 쓴 것인지 모른다. 멋모르고 지났던 처녀 시절을 보내고 과거를 뒤돌아보면 남에게 못한 일보다 아름답게 지나온 일이 더 많은 것이다. 그래서 더위가 오는 초여름까지 고운 향기로 가득 채운 것을 느끼게 한다. 시인의 삶이 바쁘게 넘쳐났지만 이웃("담장 너머엔 장미")들이 부러워할 때 시인은 달콤한 "아카시아 꽃향기"처럼 은은한 삶이었다고 노래한다.

그리고 시인은 미래를 예감한다. 초여름이 지나 가을에 상추와 쑥갓 같은 풍성함이 올 것을 짐작하고 그다음 다가오는 차가운 겨울까지 생각한다. 이러한 모든 것이 "아름다운 계절"로 승화시키고 지금 "쉬이 지치는 정신과 몸에도/여유롭게 쉬어갈 쉼터를 찾"고 있다.

In Chapter 3, poet Young Hee Han expresses not 'when **life is** hungry' but 'when hungry **for life'** in the course of her life. A meaning should be put on expressing when **hungry for** life in which the poet herself is the subject, as life is not the subject. Rather than complaining or lamenting "when hungry for life," the poet continues to think of "beautiful moments," call out "precious names," look back on the "passion that was hot like blood" of that time, and gather "courage" to draw and cultivate the future.

She captures moments of love beyond "hunger for life." Being rooted in a simple and beautiful rural life, to have love and mercy that do not disappear even though one walks various paths; life should be a natural path for a righteous person to walk.

The poet is not the kind of person who passes by indifferently to nature. Even when I look at "Pumpkin Flower," "Water Lily Blooming on the Lakeside," or "Lotus Flower," I can see that she has heart-to-heart conversations with the flowers as a poet.

After a long time of waiting
Sticking out orange lips
You came deep into my heart

한영희 시인이 살아오는 과정에서 '삶이 허기질 때'가 아니라 "삶에 허기질 때"를 제3장에서 나타내고 있다. 삶이 주체가 아니라 시인 자신이 주체가 되어 살아오는 삶에 허기질 때를 나타내는 것에 의미를 두어야 할 것이다. "삶에 허기질 때" 원망이나 한탄보다 시인은 "아름답던 순간"을 생각하며 "소중했던 이름들"을 불러보며 그 당시의 "피처럼 뜨거웠던 열정을" 돌이켜보며 오히려 "용기"를 내어 미래를 그려가며 가꾸는 것으로 이어진다.

그는 "삶에 허기"를 넘어 사랑의 순간을 포착한다. 순박하고 아름다운 시골의 삶에 뿌리를 두어 다양한 삶의 길을 걸어도 잃지 않는 사랑과 자비를 가지는 것이 올바른 사람이 걷는 당연한 길일 것이다.

시인은 자연 속에서 무심히 지나치는 성격이 아니다. 「호박꽃」 이나 「호숫가에 핀 수련」 을 보거나 「연꽃」 을 봐도 시인으로써 꽃들과 마음으로 대화를 나눈다.

오래 기다린 세월
주황색 입술 내밀며
마음 깊게 다가온 너

You open your comely and dainty mouth
With a fragrant language
To shake my heart

Having rosy passion
With a face smiling brightly
Pumpkin is ripening

Because you are full of confidence?
Or you are generous?
In response to the complaint, "Are pumpkin flowers also flowers?"
Without even blinking an eye
You smile waiting for your loved one

Even when the passing wind slightly winks
Without even looking at it
You greet the sunlight and embrace me

- Full text of "Pumpkin Flower"

Orange color has the meaning of warming the body and mind with lively energy. In particular, orange roses symbolize shyness and first love. The poet imagines the pistil of a pumpkin flower

곱살스럽고 앙증맞은 입을 열어
향기 짙은 언어로
내 마음을 흔들고 있구나

장밋빛 정열을 가진 채
활짝 웃는 얼굴로
영글어 가는 호박

자신감이 충만해서일까?
마음이 넓어서일까?
"호박꽃도 꽃이냐"는 투정에
눈 하나 꿈쩍 않고
사랑하는 이 기다리며 웃음 짓는 너

지나가는 바람이 슬쩍 윙크해도
보지도 않고
햇살을 맞이하고 나를 품는구나

- 「호박꽃」 의 전문

주황색은 활발한 기운으로 몸과 마음을 데워주는 의미를 가지고 있다. 특히 주황색 장미는 수줍음과 첫사랑의 의미를 나타내고 있다. 시인은 호박꽃의 암술이 입술을 내미는 것을 상상하며 시인의

sticking out its lips, and feels it like the kiss of first love coming deep into the poet's heart.

In addition, she gives a meaning to pumpkin flowers by saying, "You open your comely and dainty mouth/With a fragrant language/To shake my heart." Although some people may taunt about "Having rosy passion"..."With a face smiling brightly/Pumpkin is ripening" by asking, "Are pumpkin flowers also flowers?", she just expresses the happiness she feels by saying, "You greet the sunlight and embrace me." Poet Young Hee Han's poetry is a language that blooms deep in the heart and communicates with flowers. It cannot but be a beautiful heart.

Among her female siblings, poet Young Hee Han had an elder sister, who passed away, whom she loved the most. I cautiously asked her why she named her elder sister four-o'clock. The poet says that her elder sister loved the four-o'clocks blooming in the garden. She said the time her sister passed away was around 4 p.m.

Coincidentally, when I looked up the name of the flower, I found that although its scientific name is *Mirabilis jalapa* L., it is also called 'Marvel of Peru' and 'Beauty of the night' in

마음속 깊이 다가오는 첫사랑의 입맞춤과 같이 느끼고 있다.

그뿐만 아니라 "곱살스럽고 앙증맞은 입을 열어/향기 짙은 언어로/내 마음을 흔들고 있"다고 의미를 부여하고 있다. "장밋빛 정열을 가진"... "얼굴로/ 영글어가는 호박"을 때때로 "호박꽃도 꽃이냐"를 빈정대는 사람도 있겠지만 오직 "햇살을 맞이하고 나를 품는구나"라고 자신이 느끼는 행복을 토로하고 있다. 한영희 시인의 시詩는 깊은 마음속에서 피어나는 언어로서 꽃과 대화를 나눈다. 아름다운 마음이 아닐 수 없다.

한영희 시인은 여형제 가운데 가장 사랑했던 유명을 달리한 분꽃 같은 언니가 있었다. 왜 분꽃 같은 언니라고 이름을 붙였는지 조심스레 물어보았다.

시인의 언니가 정원에 피어 있는 분꽃을 너무 사랑했다고 한다.

언니가 운명한 시간도 오후 4시경이었다고 했다.

공교롭게도 필자가 분꽃의 이름을 찾아본 결과 학명이 *Mirabilis jalapa L.* 이지만 영어권 나라에서는 'Marvel of Peru', 'Beauty of the night'라고도 하는 것을 발견하였다.

English-speaking countries. What particularly caught my eye was that 'in the old days when clocks were rare, people maded inner after seeing that *Mirabilis jalapa* L bloomed around 4 p.m.' Therefore, it is said that *Mirabilis jalapa* L is also called four-o'clock in English. So, I could not but slap my knee. How could it not be a coincidence?

I heard from people around poet Young Hee Han that the poet's older sister had one son and one daughter, and that the poet devotedly took care of those children until they graduated from college and got jobs.

After that, she was late, but did not lose her desire to study, and decided to study late in life, at a university in Busan. She entered the university and completed her studies. What a beautiful story!! She is a poet who has lived accepting sacrifices.

Poet Young Hee Han titled Chapter 4 "Four-o'clock, My Elder Sister".

Precious and beautiful
My elder sister
The more I think about her, the more my heart aches.

특히 눈에 띈 것은 '예전에 시계가 귀한 때에 분꽃이 오후 4시경에 피는 것'을 보고 저녁밥을 지었다고 한다. 그래서 영어로 분꽃을 'Four-O'Clock'이라고 부르기도 한다기에 필자는 여기에 무릎을 치지 않을 수 없었다. 어찌 우연의 일치가 아닐까?

한영희 시인의 언니가 1남 1녀를 가졌는데 그 자녀들이 대학 졸업 후, 취업할 때까지 한영희 시인은 정성을 다하여 그들을 돌봐주었다는 것을 시인의 주위 사람들에게서 들었다

그 후에 늦지만 공부하고 싶은 욕망을 잃지 않고 부산의 모 대학에 늦깎이 공부를 하기 위해서 대학에 입학해서 공부를 마쳤다고 한다. 얼마나 아름다운 이야기인지 모른다. 그녀는 자기희생을 감수해 가면서도 살아온 시인이다.

한영희 시인은 제4장의 제목을 『분꽃 언니』 라고 한다.

소중하고 아름다운
나의 언니
생각할수록 가슴 저민다

When she saw the flowers, she thought it was spring and smiled.
On a lonely road where white snow falls
At the sight of her walking white
I was sad in the winter, I remember

A path we will walk together throughout our lives
She promised
I can't find it now
Only loneliness remains

Due to my heart desperately wanting to see her
With my ardent longing
I wet my eyes

Under the sunny wall
When spring comes and flowers bloom
I miss you blooming like a four-o'clock
My elder sister

- Full text of "Four-o'clock, My Elder Sister"

The content is so sad. It says that "the more I think about my "precious and beautiful" elder sister, "the more my heart aches." The elder sister she thought she would live with for a long time.

꽃을 보면 봄인 줄 알고 웃음 지었고
흰 눈 내리는 외로운 길을
하얗게 걸어가던 뒷모습에
슬펐던 겨울이 생각난다

일생동안 함께 걸어갈 길
약속 해놓고
지금은 찾아볼 수 없는
쓸쓸함만 남아 있다

보고픈 마음 간절한
애틋한 그리움에
나의 눈시울을 적신다

양지바른 담벼락 아래
봄이 와 꽃이 피면
분꽃으로 피어나는 보고픈
나의 언니

- 「분꽃 언니」 의 전문

내용이 너무 애절하다. "소중하고 아름다운" 언니가 "생각할수록 가슴 저민다"고 한다. 함께 오래도록 살아갈 줄 알았던 언니, "애틋한 그리움에/나의 눈시울을 적신다"고 말하였다. 시인은

She admits to us, “With my ardent longing/I wet my eyes.” The poet always sings, “I miss you blooming like a four-o'clock,” When spring comes and the flowers bloom.

In the poet’s poem, “Hollyhock,” she recites, “Flowers bloomed together are more beautiful than flowers bloomed alone,” and “So that even death is not fearful,” and “They find solace.” And in “Water Lily,” she says, “I live learning from you who are sitting up straight on the water.” It is believed that she wrote this poem while associating the image of the Buddha sitting upright in the Buddhist sanctuary, after seeing the water lilies blooming on the water. Religiously, as a Buddhist, she is a poet full of the mercy of Buddha.

Poet Young Hee Han unfolds the scope of her poetry with 『Scene of Ball』, in the last chapter, Chapter 5 of her poems. I feel once again that the path she has walked resembles the scene of a ball. The ball is substituted for the journey of living on the stage called, *life.*

언제나 계절이 바뀌어 다시 분꽃이 필 시기에 "분꽃으로 피어나는 보고픈/나의 언니"라고 노래하고 있다.

시인의 시편, 「접시꽃」에서 "홀로 핀 꽃보다 어울려 핀 꽃이/더욱 아름"답고, "죽음조차 두렵지 않"은 "위안을 찾는다"고 읊는다. 그리고 「수련」에서 보면 "물 위에 정좌한 너를 배우며 산다"고 한다. 아마도 물 위에 핀 수련을 보고 법당에서 부처님이 정좌한 것을 연상하며 살면서 이 시詩를 쓴 것으로 여긴다. 종교적으로도 불자로서 불심이 충만한 시인이다.

한영희 시인은 시편의 마지막 제5장을 『무도회의 풍경』으로 시詩의 영역을 펼친다. 그가 걸어온 길이 무도회의 풍경과 흡사함을 새삼 느끼고 있다. 그 무도회가 인생이라는 무대에서 살아가는 여정으로 대입한다.

As life came riding the light
The girl opened the door of crying to come out
Into a new world where even judgment is difficult

Soft skin and intelligent eyes
On the beautifully decorated stage
The entire surroundings are decorated with gems such as sapphires.

When she stands on tiptoes and spins around with white skirt,
The song of the ball is felt exciting by the young heart.

In a world that spins
With unstoppable dances
Bees and butterflies covered with faded blood come
The innocent girl needed a mask

After embroidering the clean bed sheet with beautiful passion
Eyes meeting each other dance a dance of joy
Towards an endlessly high place.

생명이 빛을 타고 들어와
판단조차 어려운 새로운 세상에
울음의 문을 열고 나온 소녀

부드러운 피부에 총명한 눈빛
예쁘게 단장된 무대에는
온통 주위가 사파이어 같은 보석으로 꾸며져 있다

발끝을 세우고 하얀 치마폭으로 한 바퀴 휙 돌면
어린 가슴에는 무도회의 노래가 흥겨워 진다

멈출 수 없는 춤으로
돌아가는 세상에
퇴색된 피를 묻혀 오는 벌·나비들
순진한 소녀는 가면이 필요했다

깨끗한 침대보에 아름다운 정열로 수놓고
맞닿는 눈길은 끝없이 높은 곳을 향하여
환희의 춤을 추기도 한다

The unstoppable waltz of the ball
In it, faces are hidden
Refinement is expressed as pretense
The sadness due to the empty dignity that is being raised.
Becomes the shame that sticks thickly
On the body that hasn't been washed for weeks

The ball still continues
Worn-out clothes and wrinkles on the crushed face
Cannot be hidden no matter how hard she tries to hide
Her sighs become a song and spread gradually

Waltz danced while holding hands at the ball
A leg standing on one toe maintains balance
And the other leg is extended fully outward and rotates,
To ride on a beautiful melody on stage.

On the stage of life where the ball comes to an end
There is nothing but regret and remorse
Oh, the conversations and the dances
Although all were thought to rise to art, but

멈출 수 없는 무도회의 왈츠
그 속에는 얼굴을 가리고
교양을 가식으로 표출하며
높여가는 공허한 품위에 서글픔은
수 주일 동안 씻지 못한 몸에
덕지덕지 붙어있는 수치심이 된다

아직도 계속되는 무도회
낡아버린 복장과 쭈그러진 얼굴의 주름
가리고 가려도 어쩔 수 없이
한숨이 노래 되어 점점 퍼지고 있다

무도회에 서로 손을 잡고 추는 왈츠
한쪽 발끝을 세운 다리가 균형을 잡고
다른 다리는 밖으로 힘껏 뻗어 회전을 하면
무대 위에서 아름다운 선율을 타게 된다

무도회가 스르르 막을 내리는 생生의 무대에는
덩그러니 후회와 회한 뿐

She is falling into a hot swamp from which she can never rise again

- Full text of "Scene of a Ball"

It would not be an exaggeration to say that the above poem is poet, Han Young-hee's, autobiographical poem. Born as a young girl, she grew up in the celebration of her entire family. The poem clearly shows that the girl has lived a life mixed with charm, as if dancing a waltz at the ball of life. There were many people who challenged her in her maidenhood, and she is talking about her journey that takes us through various times in her life thus far. When everyone looks back at the end of their life's journey, no one will feel regretful even though they may have enjoyed a beautiful life. It is true that no one can be satisfied with everything in their life. She sings of regret like this in the last verse: "On the stage of life where the ball comes to an end/There is nothing but regret and remorse/Oh, the conversations and the dances/Although all were thought to rise to art, but/She is falling into a hot swamp from which she can never rise again."

오, 대화와 춤들
모든 것이 예술로 상승할 줄 알았으나
다시는 올라오지 못할 뜨거운 늪에 빠지고 있다

- 『무도회의 풍경』의 전문

위의 시가 한영희 시인의 자서전적自敍傳的 시詩라 해도 과언이 아닐 것이다. 어린 여아로 태어나서 온 가족들이 축하 속에서 자라났다. 소녀가 인생의 무도회에서 왈츠를 추듯이 애교 섞인 생활해 옴을 잘 나타내고 있다. 쳐녀 적 자신에게 도전해 오던 여러 사람들도 있었고, 지금까지 살아온 여러 시기를 거치는 여정의 과정을 이야기 하고 있다. 인생의 여정이 끝나는 이 시점에서 누구나 뒤를 돌아보면 아름다운 생활을 누렸더라도 아쉬운 마음을 가지지 않는 사람이 없을 것이다. 누구나 인생의 삶에서 다 만족을 가질 수 없는 것이 사실이다. 그는 마지막 연에서 이렇게 아쉬움을 노래하고 있다. "무도회가 스르르 막을 내리는 생生의 무대에는/덩그러니 후회와 회한 뿐/오, 대화와 춤들/모든 것이 예술로 상승할 줄 알았으나/다시는 올라오지 못할 뜨거운 늪에 빠지고 있다"고...

These days, the majority of poetry is written in a way that makes it difficult to understand what the poet is trying to say. However, after some time passed, I think that the poetry-reading public, and even the writers who write it, begin to feel that its inherent difficulties related to expression.

The fact that a poem was written easy or with great difficulty does not mean it is not a poem. We should not insist that the poems that only the author knows, as they were written from the writer's narrow views or narrow-minded perspective, are correct. It is relative through the eyes, heart and mind of the writer (poet).

Young Hee Han's life is projected and clearly expressed in her first collection of poetry, "Scene of a Ball." The entire collection can be easily understood with all of its emotion, heart and nuance, so I think it is easy for the public to read them, while appreciating the poet's native tongue. When publishing the second collection, I hope she will produce many excellent works that can sublimate all knowledge, including ideals, philosophy, and religion, into art. I hope she will become a great poet in the genre of poetry, who is read by many readers and the public, for years and decades to come.

요즘, 쓰는 시詩가 무슨 말을 하려는지 그 내용이 난해한 글들이 주류를 이루고 있다. 그렇지만 얼마의 시간이 흐르고 나면, 시詩를 읽는 대중도 심지어 쓰는 작가조차도 난해함을 느끼게 된다고 생각한다.

쉽게 쓰거나 어렵게 쓴다고 해서 시詩가 아닌 것은 아니다. 모름지기 작가가 가지는 좁은 견해나 편협 된 시야에서 글을 쓰는 작가 자신만이 아는 시詩가 다 옳다고 고집해서는 안될 것이다.

한영희 첫 시집 "무도회의 풍경"에서 인생의 삶이 투영되어 잘 나타내고 있다. 시편 전체가 너무 어렵게 쓰이지 않아서 대중들이 읽기에 무난하다고 생각된다. 제2집을 출간할 때는 더욱더 많은 이상과 철학 그리고 종교까지 함유하는 모든 지식까지 예술로 승화시킬 수 있는 훌륭한 작품이 많이 나오기를 희망하고 있다. 시詩의 장르에서 많은 독자들이나 대중에게 읽히는 훌륭한 시인이 되기를 소망한다.

무도회의 풍경
Scene of Ball

정가 25,000원

2024년 3월 18일 인쇄
2024년 3월 21일 발행

저 자 : 한 영 희
발행인 : 박 중 열
발행처 : 다솜출판사
인쇄처 : 효성문화사

등록번호 : 1994년 4월 22일 제325-2001-000001호
부산광역시 중구 대청로 135번길 10-1
TEL : (051)462-7207/8 FAX : (051)465-0646

ISBN 978-89-5562-769-5 03810